THE WHIRLOW HALL FARM COOK BOOK

FOREWORD

WHEN WE WERE ASKED TO PROVIDE A FOREWORD FOR THIS BOOK WE THOUGHT ABOUT GETTING ONE OF THE USUAL SUSPECTS TO WRITE IT SUCH AS OUR CEO, THE CHAIR OF THE BOARD OR OUR PATRON; THEY'RE WELL-PRACTISED IN SPREADING THE WORD. BUT THEN IT OCCURRED TO US THAT WE SHOULD ASK THE FAMILY OF ONE OF THE YOUNGSTERS WE HELP INSTEAD, AND LET YOU KNOW WHAT THEY FEEL ABOUT THE TRUST. WE THINK IT WAS THE RIGHT CALL...HERE'S WHAT THEY SAID:

We were drowning and Whirlow Hall Farm Trust threw us a lifeline when we needed it most.

During the Christmas holidays of 2018, after doing a short piece for the BBC which was broadcast locally on the struggles of finding the right educational setting for our PDA* child and the lack of awareness around his particular disability, the Trust found us by way of the local village grapevine. In a world where the odds are stacked up against you, mostly due to a lack of awareness when it comes to non-visible disabilities, that phone call was the beginning of our new chapter.

The Farm has given Noah a non-judgemental setting to develop his social abilities and sense of self. It is Noah's retreat from the manic pace of the world around him, allowing him the time to learn and grow amidst the beautiful setting of the Sheffield countryside and working farm.

Whirlow's people are accepting, inclusive and understanding and have shown us a new way to nurture our fledgling who would otherwise continue to battle life's everyday demands without respite. This is something that Pathological Demand Avoidance children and adults struggle with daily, while the condition goes unrecognised.

As Mum, I am truly humbled to be asked to write this foreword and hope that the Trust may continue to blossom just as our Noah has.

With heartfelt thanks and eternal gratitude.

Diana – Noah's mum

*Pathological Demand Avoidance, part of the Autism spectrum

Diana and Noah

CONTENTS

The Whirlow Hall Farm Cook Book

©2019 Meze Publishing Ltd. All rights reserved.

First edition printed in 2019 in the UK.

ISBN: 978-1-910863-53-4

Thank you: Ben Davies and Diana Bright

Compiled by: Sarah Kerrigan

Written by: Katie Fisher

Photography by: Paul Cocker, Matt Crowder

Edited by: Phil Turner, Chris Brierley

Cover by: Sian Ellis
(www.sianellisillustration.co.uk)

Designed by: Matt Crowder, Paul Cocker

Contributors: Ruth Alexander, Marc Barker, Lydia Fitzsimons, Michael Johnson, Sarah Koriba, Mantra Media, Marek Nowicki, Sophie Westgate, Rob Whitrow

Printed by Bell and Bain Ltd, Glasgow

Published by Meze Publishing Limited
Unit 1b, 2 Kelham Square
Kelham Riverside
Sheffield S3 8SD
Web: www.mezepublishing.co.uk
Telephone: 0114 275 7709
Email: info@mezepublishing.co.uk

INTRODUCTION

Whirlow Hall Farm Trust is a beautiful place: 140 acres of green fields and dry stone walls on the hills above Sheffield. It's a proper working farm where sheep and cattle graze while looking out over the city, and hens range free. It's got a proper farm shop and a café that provides a great excuse for a rest. It's a wonderful place to take the kids or walk the dog.

But above all else, Whirlow Hall Farm Trust is an educational charity. It provides space for children and young adults to learn outside the traditional classroom environment. It focuses on children with challenges or who are disadvantaged, particularly those that struggle in mainstream education.

The trust's origins are a fascinating story and begin with Michael Hill, headmaster of Talbot School: a place for children that found the demands of mainstream education too great. He saw the benefit that outdoor activity had for pupils and so wanted to increase those opportunities for them. His first thoughts were to develop a small scale farm on spare land adjoining the school. That location proved unsuitable, but Michael was determined to find somewhere that would work. At that point fate stepped in.

Local businessman Alan Aikin wanted to repay Sheffield for the kindness it had shown him over the years and so the pair met to discuss ideas. Alan was hooked, and together they set about putting their plans into action. A list of suitable 'city' farms was drawn up, amongst them Whirlow Hall Farm. The farm was well-known to Michael – he had taken groups from Talbot School there to see the dairy in operation – and Alan, who lived locally; they knew it would be the ideal place to make the plan a reality, and in 1979 established Whirlow Hall Farm Trust.

The rest, as they say, is history. Things have evolved over time, but despite 40 years having passed, the trust remains exactly what Alan and Michael always envisaged it would be: an alternative place for disadvantaged children that struggle in mainstream education, and for children who might not otherwise be lucky enough to spend time in the countryside. For some it is an enjoyable experience, but for many it is life-changing.

Hundreds of thousands of youngsters have benefitted from the trust's work since 1979. That wouldn't have been possible without Michael Hill's vision and Alan Aikin's generosity and hard work. The trust also owes a huge debt of gratitude to the thousands of local volunteers, individuals, businesses and organisations for their support. We must also thank you for buying this cook book, which will help fund the work that we do.

Thank you.

Ben Davies, Chief Executive

(... and Esther)

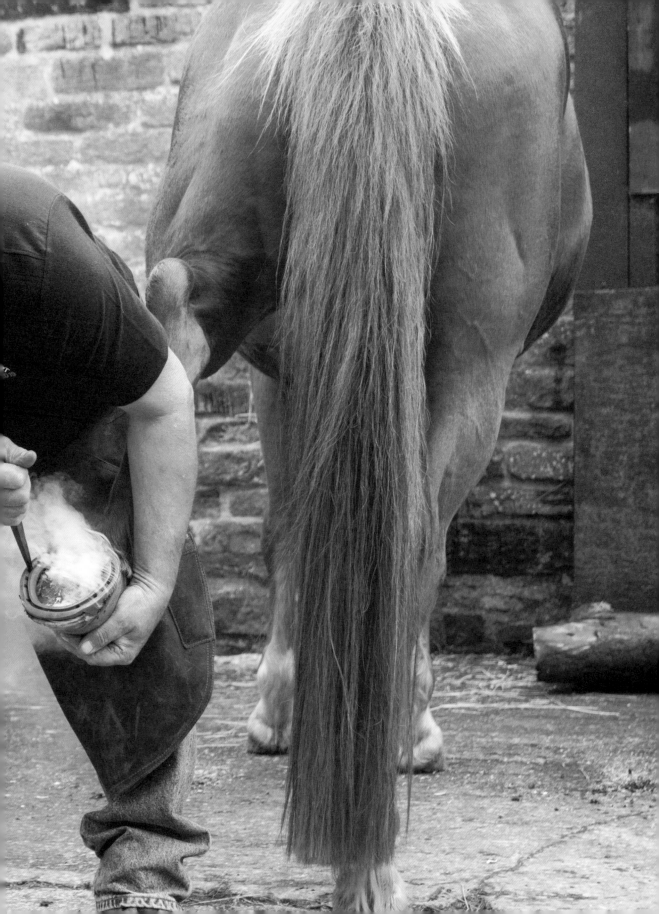

WHIRLOW HALL FARM TRUST

2019 is the 40th anniversary of Whirlow Hall Farm Trust, and in those 40 years we estimate that almost half a million school children will have visited the farm and taken part in our educational programmes. Our charitable offer has changed over the years, constantly evolving to meet the needs of the city and region, and our current focus is tackling the growing difficulties experienced by schools in ensuring there really is a place in education for every child.

We aim to inspire, nurture and expand the horizons of children and young people with social, emotional and behavioural difficulties and/or additional learning needs, many of whom struggle in school. We help to raise their aspirations, reduce their risk of social isolation and help them make the most of their potential. Our curriculum-linked activities are based on our working farm and include egg collecting, feeding the animals and pony grooming.

We run programmes for children who are excluded or at risk of exclusion from mainstream education and help them get back on track. We also run activities for young people who have additional educational needs to help them develop life skills, grow in confidence and reduce the risk of isolation. We host schools for day and residential visits so that pupils can learn in a different environment, grow in confidence and develop bonds with classmates and teaching staff. Finally, we enable college students to fulfil the practical elements of agriculture and environmental qualifications.

Our mission is to enrich the educational experience and personal development of all children and young people, regardless of their circumstances, and to improve knowledge around food, farming, and the environment. We are a classroom in the countryside. Our job is to inspire and expand horizons to give children the confidence they can achieve what they want to achieve. For many of our young visitors they have never been on a farm, so holding a freshly-hatched chick, bottle feeding a newborn lamb or seeing a pig with her piglets is an unforgettable experience. For many, it will change their lives forever.

If you would like to learn more about our work or feel able to support the Trust in any other way, please contact a member of our fundraising team via email on events@whirlowhallfarm.org or by phone on 0114 2352678. We would love to hear from you. You can also check out our website: www.whirlowhallfarm.org.

DRINKS

		Various
	Local Ales	£4·95/14·95
	House Wine	
£2·20		£2·40
£2·50		£1·50
£2·50	Posh Pop	
£2·80	San Pellegrino	
£2·00		
£2·50		£1·50

Americano
Latte
Cappuccino
Cafe Mocha
Espresso
Flat White

	£1·50
Fresh Juice	£1·00
Kids' Juice	£1/60p
Milk	

Hot Chocolate £2·50
with cream + marshmallows 60p

Ask For SOYA or OAT milk!

Tea for 1 £2·00
Tea for 2 £3·00

WiFi Password: Farm3r!!

Follow us: @WhirlowHallFarmcafe

Cheese Scones ♥♥♥

FOOD AT

WHIRLOW HALL FARM

WHIRLOW HALL FARM TRUST EMBODIES THE FIELD TO FORK APPROACH OF ETHICAL EATING. WHETHER IT'S IN THE BUTCHERY, THE FARM SHOP OR THE CAFÉ, EVERYONE WORKS TOGETHER TO CREATE DELICIOUS FOOD FROM THE FARM'S PRODUCE. THE FARM TEAM CARE FOR THE LIVESTOCK AND ENSURE IT IS IN PEAK CONDITION WHEN IT GOES TO THE ABATTOIR. THE ON-SITE BUTCHERS PRODUCE FANTASTIC CUTS OF MEAT, MAKE SAUSAGES AND CURE THEIR OWN BACON. THESE PRODUCTS ARE SOLD IN THE SHOP, OR USED BY THE KITCHEN TEAM IN THE CAFÉ TO MAKE DELICIOUS SNACKS AND MEALS. SO WHEN THE SIGN SAYS IT'S A WHIRLOW SAUSAGE ROLL OR SUNDAY ROAST, IT REALLY MEANS IT!

There's something for everyone at Whirlow Hall Farm Trust, with particular appeal for people interested in food provenance. In the café, the menu is centred around the meat reared and butchered on the farm, with an ever-changing specials board making the most of seasonal produce from the fields. The café is especially popular with young families thanks to a new children's menu that prioritises healthy eating while keeping things fun with options like snack platters.

Lamb, pork and beef served and sold at Whirlow Hall Farm is reared on the farm and prepared in the butchery. The small scale operation is unashamedly old-fashioned; whole carcass butchery, proper bacon smoking and pork pie making are dying arts. While the farm rears its own turkeys at Christmas, it doesn't yet raise chickens, so high welfare herb-fed Yorkshire chickens are sourced instead.

Whirlow Hall Farm Trust also believes that every part of an animal should be used: the most ethical approach to meat production and consumption. That belief allows the butchers to retain skills and knowledge that would otherwise die out such as rendering fat for lard, making pork scratchings, producing cured meats and so much more. Whirlow Hall Farm is the only place in Sheffield you can have pork brined, a traditional method of tenderising and preserving that has disappeared from the city over the years.

This ethos also means that the butchery and kitchen teams work in tandem, designing menus around what's available rather than ordering ingredients as a starting point. This collaboration makes for a true sense of community and teamwork. The chefs try their hand at butchery, and the butchers step into the kitchen every now and then. They work together to make the most of what the farm produces and to keep the customers happy. This friendly atmosphere extends beyond the staff, with many regular customers on first name terms with the team.

This emphasis on ethical produce is everywhere at Whirlow. The holistic approach to food production is reflected in the education programmes run by the charity. Children are taught about the whole food chain, from growing and rearing to cooking and eating.

As well as Whirlow's own produce, the farm shop also stocks preserves, flour, chocolate, honey, beer, soaps and greetings cards from small local producers. There are a few other surprises too; even the wine sold in the shop is made from grapes grown in the farm's vineyard, just 200 yards up the lane. So if you're interested in food and concerned about ethical eating, head to Whirlow!

GREEN EGGS AND HAM

This vivid and delicious brunch dish inspired by Dr. Seuss is for kids and grown ups to enjoy. The fresh green sauce completely transforms and revitalises these classic ingredients in taste as well as colour!

50g baby spinach

20g fresh parsley leaves

20g fresh basil leaves

3 tbsp grated Parmesan cheese

120ml olive oil

½ lemon, juice only

6 large eggs

Salt and pepper

2½ tbsp butter

8 slices of thick cut ham

8 slices of toast

FOR THE GREEN SAUCE

Place the spinach, parsley, basil and Parmesan in a food processor with a blade attachment. Pulse to finely chop everything. With the motor running, slowly add the oil and lemon juice to combine.

FOR THE EGGS

Crack the eggs into a bowl and whisk, adding a pinch of salt and pepper, then fold in 60ml of the green sauce (the remaining sauce can be stored in the fridge for up to 1 week).

Melt the butter in a frying pan over a low heat. Add the eggs and cook slowly, stirring constantly using a spatula until the eggs are softly set: about 10 minutes.

TO SERVE

Warm the ham through in another pan with a knob of butter while you prepare the toast. Serve the green eggs on top of the toast with two slices of ham per person on the side.

PREPARATION TIME: 20 MINUTES | COOKING TIME: 15 MINUTES | SERVES: 4

CORIANDER YORKIE WRAPS WITH LAMB KOFTAS AND TZATZIKI

This local twist on a Greek classic is packed with flavour, celebrating tastes from near and far.

FOR THE YORKIE WRAPS

4 tsp oil

140g plain flour

4 eggs

200ml milk

Salt and pepper

2 tbsp chopped fresh coriander

FOR THE KOFTAS

500g lamb mince

1 tsp ground cumin

2 tsp ground coriander

3 cloves of garlic, finely grated

1 tbsp chopped fresh mint

1 tbsp chopped fresh coriander

1 tbsp chopped fresh parsley

FOR THE TZATZIKI

300g natural yoghurt

1-2 cloves of garlic, finely grated

1 lemon, juiced

½ cucumber, grated and squeezed to remove excess water

1 tbsp chopped fresh mint

1 tbsp olive oil

Pinch of sugar

FOR THE YORKIE WRAPS

Preheat the oven to 230°c. Drizzle one teaspoon of oil into a 20cm non-stick ovenproof pan or baking dish and place in the oven to heat through.

Meanwhile, tip the flour into a large bowl and beat in the eggs until smooth. Gradually add the milk and continue beating until the mixture is completely lump-free. Season with salt and pepper then add the chopped coriander. Pour the batter into a jug.

Remove the hot pan from the oven and pour in a quarter of the batter, swirling it around so it covers the base. Return the pan to the oven and bake for 5 minutes, then flip the Yorkie wrap over and bake for another 5 minutes. Remove and repeat with the remaining oil and batter to make three more wraps.

FOR THE KOFTAS

Combine all the ingredients and season with a good pinch of salt and pepper. With wet hands, divide the mix into four and form sausage shapes. Place on a greased baking tray and cook in the oven (at the same temperature for the Yorkie wraps) for 10 to 22 minutes, until cooked through.

FOR THE TZATZIKI

Combine all the ingredients in a bowl then season to taste with salt and pepper.

TO SERVE

Dollop some tzatziki onto a warm Yorkie wrap. Top with a kofta and any other additions you choose. Here are some suggestions: a drizzle of pomegranate molasses, a scattering of pomegranate seeds, pickled cabbage, shredded lettuce, grilled halloumi, fresh herbs, a squeeze of lemon juice or a few dollops of hummus.

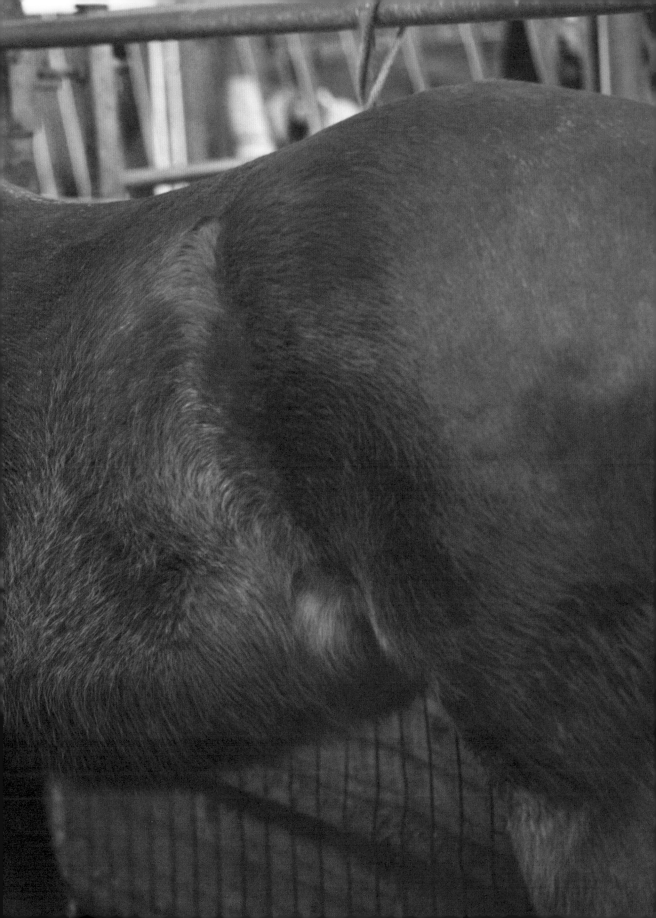

FROM THE
TINY
ANT...

THE TELESALES, TELEMARKETING AND CUSTOMER SERVICE PROVIDER, ANT MARKETING, AND ITS CHARITABLE OFFSPRING, ANT KIDS, ARE THRIVING AND PROVIDING INCREASING OPPORTUNITIES FOR SHEFFIELD PEOPLE.

Ant Marketing began life on one phone line in the founder's kitchen as a telemarketing agency, and is now a hugely successful contact centre and one of Sheffield's biggest employers. Anthony Hinchliffe established the business in 1989 and is still in the office every day as the CEO, with Sean Rawlin as his managing director and an extensive team over three city centre sites.

Because Ant Marketing works with multi-national, blue chip companies, business continues 24 hours a day and more than 30 languages are spoken collectively. Some of the partners include RBS, Heinz, Nestlé, The Economist and many more big names: the scale of the work allows Ant Marketing to currently employ over 400 people, and in 2019 alone more than 100 jobs were created with the opening of the third site for which the recruitment is ongoing.

Providing employment for the Steel City is important to Anthony – being Sheffield born and bred himself – and he has also put time and effort into helping the more disadvantaged among its population. Ant Kids is a charity set up in 2008 to support vulnerable and disadvantaged children across Sheffield. Anthony is a trustee and was joined by Account Director Holly

Fordham in 2014. The charity runs particularly big events around Christmas, making sure everyone gets the magical time they deserve no matter what their background. Looking after the local community and bringing people into the city are keystones of Ant Kids and Ant Marketing, values which they share with Whirlow Hall Farm.

"I really like the local side to Whirlow and the family-friendly element," says Holly. "It's always been a part of my life as we live very close, and every year since I was a child we have got our Christmas tree from the farm! The team there is really close-knit and very friendly, which I think makes all the difference for visitors and people benefitting from the charitable work they do."

Ant Marketing has also become the first ever corporate sponsor of Kelham Island Museum, after a vehicle of historical importance was moved there for display when Anthony 'rescued' it from being shipped out of Sheffield! Both the charity and the company are growing rapidly with even bigger ambitions and brighter prospects for the future, in the context of a firm ongoing commitment to Sheffield and its people.

ant marketing

antenna house
reception

focused

SLOW COOKED BEEF MASSAMAN CURRY

I've loved curries since I was a child: Thai, Indian, Chinese or any other kind! I first tried massaman curry in Bali a few years ago and decided to recreate one for my blog, Hollywould Food. After a few trials, I decided this was the perfect version. Hope you enjoy it!

FOR THE CURRY

1kg beef, cut into chunks (braising is fine, but I use rump steaks)

Salt and pepper

Cornflour

1 tbsp coconut oil (or vegetable oil if not available)

1 large brown onion, as finely diced as possible

3 fresh chillies (Scotch Bonnets if you like it hot!), finely chopped

2½cm fresh ginger, grated

1 level tsp ground cinnamon

3 tbsp massaman paste

570ml (1 pint) weak beef stock (2 stock cubes is perfect)

1 tin of reduced fat coconut milk

3 large white potatoes, peeled and cut into large chunks

TO SERVE

Sticky jasmine rice

1 fresh chilli, thinly sliced

Desiccated coconut

Fresh lime

Season the beef with salt and pepper and then toss in enough cornflour to coat each piece. Heat the coconut oil then fry the beef for approximately 5 minutes, or until they all start to brown. This can be done in batches if easier, depending on the size of your pan.

Turn on your slow cooker and set at a low heat (130°c is perfect). If you don't have a slow cooker, you can use a large ovenproof dish with a lid in a preheated oven. While the slow cooker or oven is heating up, add the onion, chilli, fresh ginger and ground cinnamon to the beef. Cook for a further 5 minutes.

Add the massaman paste to the pan and stir to coat everything with it before transferring the mixture to the slow cooker (be sure to scrape the bottom of the pan for all the stuck-on flavour). Pour the beef stock over the mixture and add half of the coconut milk. Stir so everything is combined before putting the lid on. Leave to cook for around 2 and a half to 3 hours, stirring occasionally. If it sticks at any stage, just add a little water to prevent anything from burning.

Add the peeled and chopped potatoes to the curry along with the rest of the coconut milk. Stir to combine and cover with the lid. The potatoes should take around 1 hour to cook, but test at 45 minutes and again at 1 hour. They need to be tender but this can vary depending on size. Again, add water if necessary.

Serve the curry with sticky jasmine rice and top with thinly sliced fresh chilli, a sprinkling of desiccated coconut and a wedge of fresh lime for each person.

PREPARATION TIME: 10 MINUTES | COOKING TIME: 4 HOURS | SERVES 4-6

B HEALTHY

B. BRAUN IS A COMPANY FOCUSED ON THE BENEFITS OF A HEALTHIER LIFESTYLE, ESPECIALLY FOR YOUNG PEOPLE, AND SUBSEQUENTLY WORKS WITH CHARITIES LIKE WHIRLOW HALL FARM TO MAKE A DIFFERENCE IN SHEFFIELD.

With over 64,000 employees in 64 countries, B. Braun is one of the world's leading manufacturers of medical devices and pharmaceutical products and services. B. Braun develops high quality product systems and services that are both evolving and progressive, and in turn improves people's health around the world.

The B. Braun Medical UK Headquarters is based at Thorncliffe Park in Sheffield and, via the Employee Forum Members, has supported Whirlow Hall Farm for a number of years. It offers marketing support and promotional materials which feature on the website, along with more practical support such as the provision of hand sanitiser around the farm. As part of the corporate mission – to protect and improve the health of people around the world – B. Braun delivered a state-of-the-art defibrillator to Whirlow Hall Farm Trust, supported by a training programme for the volunteers on how to use the equipment. This was well received not only by the staff, volunteers and visitors, but also by the local community as Whirlow made the equipment accessible to all their neighbours in the village.

B. Braun are also active members of the Whirlow Hall Farm 480 Club, and have enthusiastically supported the various activities associated with the membership. When the B. Braun Employee Forum heard about this cook book, they were particularly interested in making a contribution as it complements the activities that are part of the 'B. Healthy B. Braun' health and wellbeing initiative, working alongside the B. Braun Sheffield Sharks Basketball Club. The programme is an inventive approach to addressing inactivity in young people within local communities and aims to educate young people in leading a healthier lifestyle, the importance of good nutrition and being active, to help them understand how lifestyle behaviours, diet and exercise can impact their lives. Some of the children who visit Whirlow will have attended 'B. Healthy B. Braun' events at their schools.

The recipes which have been chosen for the following pages take a naturally healthy approach to tasty family-friendly recipes. There is an interesting lunch box option which can be made together, and a family tea time meal for everyone to eat while sitting and socialising around the table! "We hope that you enjoy both recipes, and that together with Whirlow Hall Farm we can continue to support our local communities."

CRISPY CHICKEN SCHNITZEL

This delicious recipe for chicken schnitzel involves coating the chicken with wholewheat breadcrumbs and baking it in the oven using cooking spray instead of frying in lots of oil. A great recipe for the whole family to enjoy, which can easily be converted to a vegetarian or vegan meal using meat-free products.

Olive oil cooking spray

2 225g boneless skinless chicken breasts, trimmed, or 4 Quorn fillets

½ tsp salt

½ tsp freshly ground pepper

30g white wholewheat flour

2 large eggs, beaten

1 lemon, zested

250g fresh wholewheat breadcrumbs

30g fresh herbs, chopped (such as dill, parsley and chives)

Preheat the oven to 230°c. Coat a large baking sheet with the cooking spray.

Cut the chicken breasts in half horizontally or use whole Quorn fillets. Cover the fillets with a large piece of cling film and pound with the smooth side of a meat mallet or a heavy saucepan to an even half centimetre thickness. Sprinkle the chicken with half of the salt and pepper (quarter of a teaspoon each).

Place the flour in one shallow dish and the beaten eggs in another. Combine the lemon zest with the breadcrumbs and herbs in a third shallow dish. Coat both sides of the chicken in the flour, shaking off any excess, then dip in egg, and finally coat on both sides with the breadcrumbs, pressing gently to help them stick. Place the chicken on the prepared baking sheet and coat on both sides with cooking spray. Bake the chicken in the preheated oven until golden brown and no longer pink in the centre. This should only take 10 to 12 minutes. If you are using Quorn, follow the cooking guidelines on the packet.

Serve the schnitzel with mixed greens, mashed potato or vegetables of your choice.

PREPARATION TIME: 20 MINUTES | COOKING TIME: 20 MINUTES | SERVES: 4

RAINBOW WRAPS

A quick and easy rainbow vegetable wrap that you can make with the kids. Packed full of colourful crunchy veggies, the kids will love getting involved in making these healthy, budget friendly lunchbox favourites. Top tip: make sure the vegetables are dry so you don't get soggy wraps.

8 tortilla wraps

2 carrots, cut into batons

150g red cabbage, sliced or shredded

1 red pepper, deseeded and sliced

½ cucumber, cut into batons

Handful of spinach leaves (or other greens)

200g hummus

Handful of chives (or other herbs)

Spread out the tortilla wraps, and add as much of each vegetable as you like.

Top with a generous serving of hummus and some chopped herbs, wrap the tortilla and serve.

You can use any leftover vegetables that you have in the fridge, and swap ingredients to keep it interesting. You could also use peanut butter or other dips instead of hummus.

Please supervise children when using a grater or knife.

PREPARATION TIME: 10 MINUTES | SERVES: 4

SCHOOL
DINNERS
REIMAGINED

BIRKDALE SCHOOL OFFERS THE HIGHEST STANDARDS IN EVERYTHING IT DOES, AND WANTS EVERY CHILD TO BE THE BEST THEY CAN BE. PUPILS RECEIVE AN OUTSTANDING, WELL-ROUNDED EDUCATION WHICH IS ENHANCED BY THEIR EXCELLENT SCHOOL MEALS, PROVIDED BY A CATERING TEAM WHO ENSURE THAT STUDENTS HAVE HEALTHY, VARIED AND TASTY LUNCHES EVERY DAY.

Birkdale School has a long and distinguished history. Res Non Verba – Actions Not Words – is the motto, and throughout its history the school has certainly lived up to this. Forward thinking and continually evolving, Birkdale meets the needs of the modern world with dedicated teachers delivering an outstanding well-rounded education. Today, Birkdale specialises in quality education for children aged 4 to 16, with a thriving co-educational Sixth Form which prepares young adults for higher education.

Academic success is only part of the story. The school offers an enormous range of extra-curricular opportunities to recognise and nurture individual talents in sports, music, drama or outdoor pursuits. Across Birkdale – whether at Prep School, Senior School or Sixth Form – the standard of pastoral care is exceptionally high. This creates a warm, caring and supportive environment with excellent relationships between students and teachers. The dynamic curriculum focuses on academic ambition, achieved through a well-rounded education and backed up by Christian values.

This ethos extends to every aspect of school life, including the daily lunches. Birkdale wants pupils to be well fed, and teachers' feedback shows that performance is significantly better after a good meal. The emphasis is on healthy eating, and a key trend is the vegetarian dishes which are currently very popular. The wide range of options covers soups, a salad bar, hot dishes, jacket potatoes, desserts and drinks for a well-balanced meal every day. Wilson Vale Catering have been employed by Birkdale School for nearly ten years, and the head chef, Chris Allison, formerly worked at The Cavendish Hotel in Baslow, so he knows how important great produce is too, sourcing nutritious ingredients to form the basis of all the dishes.

Birkdale School is proud to enjoy such amazing food, and to support other organisations that share the drive to help children eat well and be their best. Whirlow Hall Farm has a strong link with Birkdale in this respect, and many of the school's pupils visit the farm and have connections with the charitable work. As an independent, self-funded institution, Birkdale School takes on a duty to give back to the community, offering bursaries and supporting local charities like Whirlow to improve young people's lives through education and everything else that contributes to their wellbeing.

RICOTTA AND SPINACH TORTILLA CANNELLONI

The traditional pasta tubes have been replaced with tortilla wraps in this recipe for a more 'on trend' twist. A good tip is to use the piping bag to place the required amount of filling on each wrap before rolling, making it quicker and easier to produce lots of food for hungry children and teenagers!

FOR THE CANNELLONI

Knob of butter

6 shallots, peeled and diced

300g baby spinach, washed

500g ricotta cheese

2 eggs

FOR THE TOMATO SAUCE

3 tbsp olive oil

3 cloves of garlic, peeled and finely chopped

800g tinned chopped tomatoes

100ml vegetable stock

1 tsp sugar

2 tsp distilled vinegar

TO FINISH

8 25cm tortilla wraps

125g vegetarian Italian hard cheese, grated

Small bunch of fresh basil, roughly chopped

FOR THE CANNELLONI

Heat a frying pan, add the knob of butter, gently fry the shallots and wilt the spinach, then leave to cool.

Using an electric mixer with a paddle attachment, slowly beat the ricotta and eggs together, then add the cooled spinach and shallots. This can be done by hand if required. The spinach can be chopped before cooking to make it easier to incorporate. Set aside while you make the sauce.

FOR THE TOMATO SAUCE

Heat the olive oil in a medium-sized pan. Add the garlic and cook for 1 minute, then add all the other ingredients. Cook over a moderate heat for a further 10 to 12 minutes. Add a little hot water if the sauce gets too thick.

TO FINISH

Pipe the ricotta and spinach mixture along the centre of each wrap. Roll up and place side by side in an ovenproof dish. Cover the wraps with the tomato sauce and bake for 30 minutes at 160°c, then top with the grated hard cheese, turn the oven up to 190°c and bake for a further 5 minutes until melted on top. Serve with a scattering of chopped basil or a drizzle of basil oil.

PREPARATION TIME: 20 MINUTES | COOKING TIME: 40 MINUTES | SERVES 4-6

SHEFFIELD'S DELICIOUSLY DIVERSE

MELTING POT

BLEND KITCHEN IS A SOCIAL ENTERPRISE IN THE FORM OF A CAFÉ AND RESTAURANT, RUN BY A CHEF WHO DECIDED TO PUT HIS UNIQUE COMBINATION OF SKILLS TO GOOD USE.

Chris Hanson founded Blend Kitchen in 2018 following a career in the restaurant industry, and a desire to help improve people's health and wellbeing through teaching and creating opportunities for work experience and skill building. He was involved in Sharrow Community Forum, a membership organisation which inspired Chris to develop a self-sustainable way of reaching the people who needed it most, without relying on decreasing funding. He was joined by Joanna Rutter and Gareth Jones, both directors on a volunteer basis alongside their full-time jobs which give them the relevant experience and aptitude to help Blend continue its journey.

Everything at Blend is based around food, from cookery classes in primary schools to community events. These initiatives take place across Sheffield and aim to help vulnerable or disadvantaged people by giving them the ability and knowledge to cook for themselves in sheltered housing, for example, or realise their potential by taking up a placement at the café and restaurant itself. The staff come from a wide range of backgrounds and cultures, but all want to learn new skills or get into the catering industry. Chris draws inspiration from this eclectic mix to dream up the menus, reflecting the many cuisines that exist in Sheffield as well as celebrating local producers by using their ingredients.

Little Mesters Cheesemakers, Abbeydale Brewery, Robin of Locksley gin distillers and Whirlow Hall Farm are some of the nearest suppliers, ensuring top quality at Blend Kitchen.

With new specials every day and a bi-monthly makeover for the main menus, there's never a dull dish at the café and restaurant. Chris regularly invites guest chefs and cooks to cater for themed evenings as diverse as Taiwanese, Romanian and Antiguan. The international outreach even extends to the coffee menu, which was developed in partnership with the kitchen's two suppliers, Pollards and Twin Café, which imports coffee produced by a worker's co-operative from a town in Nicaragua twinned with Sheffield. Other hot drinks are sourced from Birdhouse Tea, perfect for enjoying with dessert which are all made by volunteers at The Archer Project.

By offering delicious food and drink – all freshly prepared on site or locally – to eat in or take away, Chris is able to fund the important work that Blend Kitchen exists to make possible. His café and restaurant is an opportunity for fresh starts, a hub for great Yorkshire produce, and a place to enjoy diverse dishes that make a difference.

Photos: Mantra Media

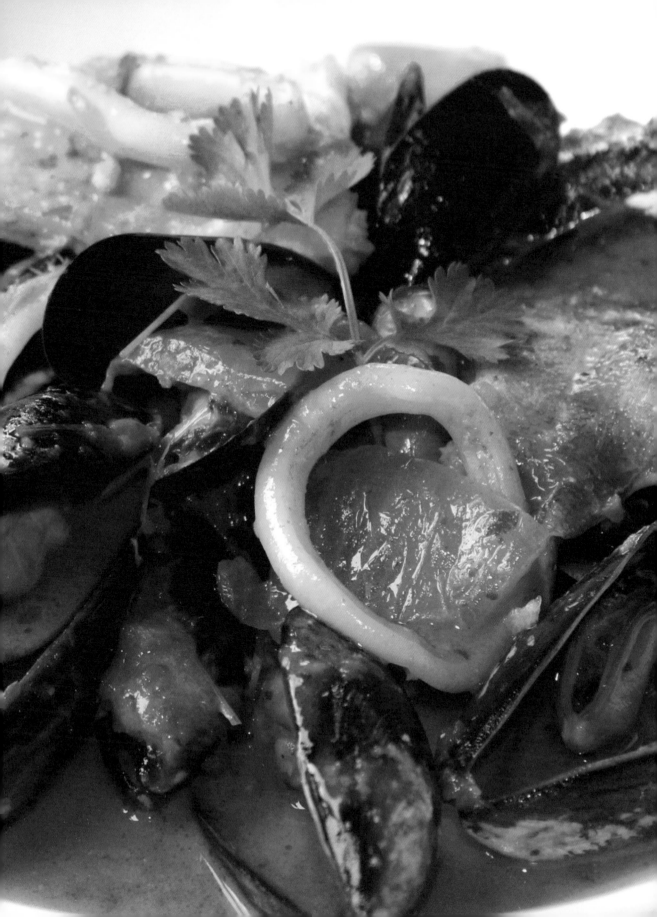

MOROCCAN FALAFEL WRAPS

This dish combines some of the most well-known and delicious flavours of the middle east and North Africa to create an affordable, vegetarian meal.

FOR THE FALAFEL

1 jar of roasted peppers
1 tin of chickpeas, drained
2 tbsp cumin seeds, toasted
1 tbsp sumac powder
1 lemon, zest and juiced
1 bunch of fresh coriander, chopped
2 tbsp gram flour
Salt and pepper
Olive oil

FOR THE SALADS

1 head of broccoli
1 jar of harissa
1 bunch of heritage carrots
1 tbsp cumin seeds
1 orange, juiced

FOR THE HUMMUS

1 tin of chickpeas
1 tbsp each of cumin and coriander seeds
1 tbsp tahini
4 cloves of garlic, peeled and crushed
½ lemon, juiced

FOR THE TABBOULEH

1 tsp ground cumin
1 tsp ground coriander
1 tsp ground cinnamon
500g couscous
Fresh herbs of your choice (we like mint, coriander, parsley and dill)
½ lemon, juiced
1 chilli, finely diced

TO SERVE

Wraps or flatbreads of your choice
Fresh coriander, roughly chopped
Plain or Greek-style yoghurt
Chilli sauce of your choice

FOR THE FALAFEL

Blitz the roasted peppers to a purée using a blender, then stir in the chickpeas. Add the cumin seeds and sumac, lemon zest and juice, coriander, gram flour and a little salt and pepper. Mix to combine everything thoroughly, then fry a small piece until cooked to check the seasoning and consistency. Roll the falafel mixture into even-sized balls and place them in the fridge for 30 minutes. To cook the falafel, fry the balls in oil at 180°c.

FOR THE SALADS

Split the head of broccoli into florets and blanch them in boiling water, then drain well. Heat some oil in a frying pan, add the broccoli and harissa, cook until just done and finish with a drizzle of olive oil and seasoning.

Blanch the carrots for 4 minutes in boiling water, then refresh them in cold water and drain. Toast the cumin seeds then mix them with the orange juice and some olive oil. Season with salt and pepper then toss the carrots in the dressing until they are well coated.

FOR THE HUMMUS

Drain the tin of chickpeas and put them in a blender. Toast the cumin and coriander seeds then add them to the blender along with the tahini, garlic, lemon juice and some olive oil. Blitz the mixture to a smooth purée.

FOR THE TABBOULEH

Bring 500ml of water to the boil with the ground cumin, coriander and cinnamon. Pour this over the couscous, cover with cling film or a plate, then leave to stand for 5 minutes. Combine with herbs, olive oil, lemon juice, chilli, salt and pepper.

TO SERVE

Warm the wraps and then fill each one with hummus, tabbouleh, dressed carrots and harissa-glazed broccoli. Finish with crispy falafel, fresh coriander, yoghurt, and chilli sauce.

PREPARATION TIME: 30 MINUTES | COOKING TIME: 30 MINUTES | SERVES: 4

YOUR FRIENDLY
NEIGHBOURHOOD KITCHEN

BROCCO KITCHEN IS ALWAYS SEASONAL, A LITTLE BIT SCANDINAVIAN AND UNMISTAKEABLY SHEFFIELD...

From breakfast to dinner, the 'neighbourhood kitchen' at Brocco on the Park offers a smorgasbord of delicious freshly made food to enjoy at any time of the day, for locals as well as hotel guests. Brocco Kitchen was established in 2014, with head chef Leslie Buddington at the helm since the beginning. Each season, Leslie and his team plan the menus around the available produce to build dishes that are bursting with flavour and full of goodness. "Eating is all about balance," says Leslie, "so if you make healthy choices, you can have your cake and eat it!"

Because everything is made in-house with fresh ingredients, the menu is generally a healthy one whether you're after a hearty breakfast, light lunch or refreshing smoothie on a summer day. The morning options are always popular, and include classic egg dishes, indulgent topped waffles and big plates for meat, fish and vegetable lovers. Staying for the smorgasbord, served at midday (12.30pm at weekends) and evening (except Sundays), will present you with an exciting range of small plates across the same 'Hunter', 'Fisher' and 'Gardener' sections that pair tried and tested flavour combinations with inventive methods and a touch of luxury. Afternoon tea comes in between: a treat from the finger sandwiches to the dainty sweets that includes specialist loose leaf teas and filter coffee.

Sunday roast specials, banquets for gatherings, the specially designed kids' menu and your favourite tipple – from morning mimosas to classy cocktails – make Brocco Kitchen a go-to whenever you fancy eating out with the family, celebrating a big occasion with friends, or impressing a date! The team go out of their way to make Brocco Kitchen welcoming for every one of the huge mix of guests that visit. The ethos revolves around feeling at home, enjoying laid back dining, encouraging people to share and generally creating a great atmosphere that's much more relaxed than you might expect to find in a hotel restaurant.

Brocco Kitchen has already been featured in the Michelin Guide several times, won lots of awards, and got involved with local competitions including Sheff's Kitchen at Whirlow Hall Farm. Leslie had always been interested in working with the charity, and the opportunity arose when he was asked to join the Sheff's Kitchen line-up in 2019. "It's a great thing they're doing up there," says Leslie, "and I'm excited to now be a part of that and represent the food I love creating here at Brocco Kitchen."

BEEF CHEEK, CELERIAC AND WENSLEYDALE COTTAGE PIE

This tender beef cheek in its aromatic sauce is a great recipe to impress the family with. Combined with the earthy celeriac and tangy Wensleydale cheese it's always a winner at the table. Chef's tip: add an egg yolk to the mashed potato for a richer mash.

Vegetable oil

4 ox cheeks

3 carrots

3 white onions

1 leek

2 celery sticks

3 cloves of garlic

1 tsp tomato purée

½ bunch of thyme

1 bay leaves

½ stick of cinnamon

2 star anise

1 large glass red wine

2 litres beef stock

FOR THE CELERIAC MASH

2 celeriac

4 small Maris Piper potatoes

100g butter

50ml milk

Salt and pepper

TO FINISH

200g Wensleydale cheese

Preheat the oven to 150°c. Place a little vegetable oil in a hot pan and seal the ox cheeks on both sides until well browned, then remove from the pan. In the same pan, cook the carrots, onions, leek, celery and garlic until golden brown, then add the tomato purée and cook for a few minutes. Add the thyme, bay leaves, cinnamon, star anise and red wine then reduce the liquid by half.

Transfer the ox cheek, vegetables and wine into a casserole dish and add the beef stock. Cover the dish with greaseproof paper and tin foil, then place in the preheated oven to cook for 3 hours until the meat is really tender and falling apart.

Take the cheeks out of the liquid and shred the meat into pieces. Strain the cooking liquor through a fine sieve into a saucepan, place on a medium heat and reduce the liquid by half.

While the liquor is reducing, start the celeriac mash. Peel the celeriac and potatoes, then cut into similar sizes to ensure they cook at the same time. Place the potatoes and celeriac into a pan of salted water and bring to the boil. Cook until soft. Drain the celeriac and potatoes then mash them together, adding the butter and milk a little at a time. Season to taste with salt and pepper.

Once the liquor has reduced and thickened, add the shredded beef to the sauce. Transfer this into the casserole dish and top with a layer of celeriac mash. Grate the Wensleydale cheese over the top and bake the cottage pie at 180°c for 25 to 30 minutes.

PREPARATION TIME: 20 MINUTES | COOKING TIME: 3½ HOURS | SERVES: 6

THE BEST OF

LAND & SEA

BUTCHER & CATCH IS ALL ABOUT SUPPORTING PRODUCERS, FARMERS AND SUPPLIERS IN SHEFFIELD AND SOUTH YORKSHIRE, WHOSE FANTASTIC PRODUCE IS SHOWCASED IN THE SEASONAL MENUS AT THE RESTAURANT.

The family-run business based in Broomhill opened in October 2017, aiming to provide a really accessible dining experience where there's something for everyone on the menu. Owners Liam and Adam embrace the wonderful produce that's grown, reared and created throughout Sheffield and South Yorkshire. "We are blessed to have so much in the area, including breweries and distilleries, and it's important to recognise and celebrate that," says Liam. This ethos underpins everything about Butcher & Catch, from the upcycled feel of the restaurant interiors to the food menus.

All the dishes are based on seasonality, which includes drawing inspiration not only from what's on offer at certain times of the year, but also what people want to eat in different weathers and what reflects the local supply chain. Staples such as steak and oysters are firm favourites, but fish in particular will change regularly as Butcher & Catch uses only sustainable produce and the varieties available in our own waters depend completely on the time of year. Head chef Chris encapsulates this approach in his food by always looking ahead to keep the menu fresh and exciting for returning customers. "One of the difficult parts of creating a seasonal menu is when you're sat in the summer sun trying to imagine warming autumnal dishes for the next season!" says Liam.

You'll find the same level of attention to detail in the selection of drinks throughout the year; stouts in the winter and fruity beers during warmer months are broad examples of how closely Liam and his team stick to seasonal flavours and ingredients. Everything from Sheffield breweries is on tap at Butcher & Catch, and the restaurant plays host to events in collaboration with the likes of Sir Robin of Locksley gin to give customers a taste of the city's artisanal tipples. Good relationships with these producers and suppliers allow the restaurant to work on great food and drink pairings, creating flavours from all over the world with ingredients sourced on the doorstep. "Artisanal and creative local produce, which has been created and crafted with love is our top priority when sourcing the products for our seasonal menus. The focus and priority has, and always will be, to use local suppliers who put a great deal of care and attention into the food and drinks that we serve every day."

SURF AND TURF

These oysters with granita are light and refreshing and a great way to start a meal. You can try whichever gins and tonics you like for this recipe but stick to the quantities as alcohol affects the freezing process. The hearty cut of meat to follow is one our favourites, full of flavour and always a crowd pleaser. We find a hoppy pale ale works best for the sauce.

FOR THE G&T OYSTERS

12 oysters

50ml gin (brand and flavour is optional)

200ml tonic water

1 tsp caster sugar

FOR THE BBQ BEEF SHORT RIBS

1 tbsp mixed spice

½ tbsp salt (preferably sea salt)

½ tbsp garlic powder

1 tbsp onion powder

¼ tbsp ground black pepper

1 tbsp smoked paprika

2 tbsp dark brown sugar

4 beef short rib portions

570ml (1 pint) hoppy ale

300ml BBQ sauce

200ml beef stock

FOR THE MUSTARD MASH

1kg Maris Piper potatoes

75g butter

2 tbsp wholegrain mustard

TO SERVE

2 limes, cut into wedges

Crispy onions (optional)

FOR THE G&T OYSTERS

Shuck the oysters and remove any bits of shell or dirt. Mix the gin and tonic with the sugar. We used Sir Robin of Locksley gin and Fentiman's Pink Grapefruit Tonic Water. Decant into a small container and place in the freezer for about 1 hour, then scrape the crystals from around the edge with a fork and stir them in. Freeze again and repeat this process after 1 hour so the granita is fluffy and crystalized, then keep in the freezer until needed.

FOR THE BBQ BEEF SHORT RIBS

Preheat the oven to 130°c then mix together the dry ingredients and rub generously over the ribs. Combine the ale, BBQ sauce and beef stock in a deep tray or ovenproof dish. Place the ribs in the sauce bone side down and cover the whole dish with tin foil (if the tin foil is touching the meat, place a sheet of greaseproof paper in between to stop it sticking). Place the ribs in the preheated oven and cook for 4 to 5 hours, or until the meat is tender and nearly falling off the bone.

Carefully remove the ribs from the tray and set aside. Pour the sauce into a saucepan and reduce over a gentle heat until it thickens and starts to get sticky. Place the ribs back into the tray and pour the sauce over them. Keep warm until serving.

FOR THE MUSTARD MASH

Peel the potatoes and cut them into evenly sized pieces. Cook in a pan of boiling water for about 15 to 20 minutes or until tender. Drain in a colander and leave for a few minutes to allow any excess water to drain away. Tip the potatoes back into the pan and mash well with the butter until smooth. Mix in the mustard and season with salt and pepper if needed.

TO SERVE

For your starter, place the prepared oysters on a serving tray covered with ice and top each one with the granita. Garnish with the fresh lime wedges.

For your main course, scoop a portion of mash onto four warm plates and place the ribs bone side down onto the plate leaning up against the mash. Spoon some of the sauce over the ribs and sprinkle with crispy onions.

PREPARATION TIME: 10 MINUTES, 2-3 HOURS FOR FREEZING | SERVES 3-4
PREPARATION TIME: 15-20 MINUTES | COOKING TIME: 5-6 HOURS | SERVES 4

MEAT

THE
MAKER

HAVING OPENED A SECOND SHOP AND STRENGTHENED A FRUITFUL RELATIONSHIP WITH WHIRLOW HALL FARM, CHRIS BEECH QUALITY MEATS IS THRIVING AMIDST ITS SUPPORT AND PROMOTION OF OTHER LOCAL ENTERPRISES.

Chris Beech took over a small butcher's shop in Walkley in 2010, which he has run with his wife Donna ever since to growing success. The meat counter is a prominent feature, showcasing local produce as well as more unusual cuts not easily found elsewhere. There is also an incredible range of handmade sausages – which now comprises over 50 varieties, a dozen of which are award-winning – plus burgers and dry-cured bacon too. The combination of pork from Whirlow Hall Farm, honey from The Sheffield Honey Company and Chris' own mustard proved a particular favourite in 2018's UK Sausage Week, which gave it a gold award, and the 'Sheffield Secret Sausage' is one of Chris' most popular creations, thanks in part to its mysterious local ingredient...Henderson's Relish, of course!

Fulwood Road welcomed the arrival of Chris Beech's second shop in 2017 where the same range is available, even closer to an important supplier: Whirlow Hall Farm. All the sausages are now made with Whirlow produce, and Chris turns the farm's pork, beef and lamb into products which are sold not only in his shops and at the farm, but by other butchers in Sheffield that he supplies. The partnership has been well established for several years, and Chris has done some demonstrations at the farm with the products he makes for them. "Whirlow does such a lot to help families and young people, and it's also really good for the food industry, because it educates people about where their meat and veg comes from and how to use it properly," says Chris.

Supporting and promoting local businesses and charities is really important to Chris and Donna, and one of the reasons they opened in Walkley was to revitalise the high street and draw people back to the wonderful food created in their area. The shop sells Sheffield honey, jams, chutneys, sauces, ice cream and other dairy from Our Cow Molly, and also has an eco-friendly section of frozen fruits, vegetables and pastries which are packaging-free. This also applies to the meat, as customers are encouraged to bring their own containers to reduce plastic waste. From Donna's hand-painted farm mural in the Walkley shop to the many local gems you can find within it, Chris Beech Quality Meats continues to be a hub for Sheffield food lovers.

PICNIC PARTY SANDWICH LOAF

No party or picnic was complete without NanNan Judy's family favourite.
We now use Whirlow Hall Farm free-range eggs and high welfare pork in
the recipe, which can only make our loaf tastier!

1 small crusty bloomer loaf

85g fresh white breadcrumbs (from the loaf)

85g butter, melted

225g sausage meat

55g onions, peeled and chopped

¼ tsp dried sage

1 egg, beaten

3 tbsp milk

Salt and pepper

2-3 eggs, hard boiled

Preheat the oven to 200°c.

Cut horizontally across the loaf, two thirds of the way up. Remove the "lid" and gently ease the bread away from the crust. Make the breadcrumbs from the soft crumb. Brush the cavity and lid with some of the melted butter.

Combine the sausage meat with the chopped onion, sage, egg, milk and seasoning. Place a third of the sausage meat mixture in the centre of the loaf. Arrange the hard boiled eggs down the middle, pack the rest of the filling around them, then top with the lid.

Secure with strips of foil and brush the loaf with the remaining melted butter. Bake in the preheated oven on a baking sheet for 15 minutes, then cover completely with foil and bake for a further 45 minutes.

Serve warm or cold, cut into thick slices.

PREPARATION TIME: 15 MINUTES | COOKING TIME: 60 MINUTES | SERVES: 8-10

REPRESENTING SHEFFIELD

CMS IS ONE OF THE TOP CORPORATE LAW FIRMS IN THE WORLD, AND THE SHEFFIELD OFFICE HAS BEEN A KEY PART OF THE FIRM'S DEVELOPMENT UP TO AND CONTINUING FROM THE MERGER OF LEGACY FIRM NABARRO WITH CMS AND OLSWANG IN 2017.

The firm has had an office in Sheffield since 1990, first establishing roots in the city when its legacy firm acquired the legal team from British Coal Corporation.

As a major international firm CMS works with large corporations and clients from around the world. Despite this, the 250 plus employees in the Sheffield office are all local, including over 150 lawyers who advise local, national and international clients on a wide range of matters, including real estate, banking and finance, clinical and professional risk, corporate, construction, employment, environment, health and safety, pensions, planning, and disputes.

CMS has always been proud of its connection with Sheffield, and sees itself as an important part of the city's business landscape. "They have seen Sheffield City Region develop markedly in recent years. The region is ambitious and keen to expand its role as a major hub for business, as well as an attractive place to live, work and visit," says CMS partner Mark Haywood. "Sheffield is attracting investment from all over the world, so knowing that we are part of that development is a great thing."

CMS is proud to work closely with organisations that provide support to the city's economy and people, including Whirlow Hall Farm, for whom former partner Martin McKervey is a trustee.

CMS is a bit of a foodie hotspot too. Led by chef Michael Davies, a catering team works every day to prepare lunch served in the staff canteen and also creates some of the best food in the city at the numerous client dinners and events held on site during the year. It's been said that an army marches on its stomach... it must be the same for lawyers!

DRESSED SALMON, BEETROOT, CUCUMBER & LEMON PURÉE

This dish came about as a result of CMS hosting an annual dinner for local businesswomen to mark International Women's Day. The organisers requested a starter that was light and looked funky on the plate but featured flavours that people know and recognise. This tasty and colourful dish was the result and it's now become a firm favourite.

500g salmon fillet

1 onion

1 carrot

Bouquet garni (bay, thyme, dill)

Large pinch of salt

½ lemon, sliced

Few sprigs of dill

10 capers

2 tbsp crème fraîche

Squeeze of lemon juice

Pinch of salt

4 red beetroot

Olive oil

2-3 sprigs of thyme

100ml white wine vinegar

50ml water

2 tbsp sugar

1 cucumber

2 lemons

4 tbsp water

2 tbsp honey

Pinch of salt

20 capers

Trim the salmon by cutting away the thin belly piece and any untidy bits, and keep the trimmings to one side. Divide the salmon into four 100g square portions.

Chop the onion and carrot, put in a pot with the bouquet garni and salt, cover with water and boil for 10 minutes. Lower the heat, add the salmon portions and trimmings, then very gently poach for 4 to 5 minutes until just firm. Add the sliced lemon then allow to cool completely.

Prepare the rillettes by removing the salmon trimmings from the liquor and flaking them into a bowl. Add the dill, capers, crème fraîche, lemon juice and seasoning. Mix gently.

Wrap the beets in foil with a splash of oil, thyme and seasoning. Bake at 180°c until a knife will slide in (approximately 1 hour). Cool, skin and cut two of the beets into cubes or discs.

Prepare the pickling liquor by gently warming the vinegar, water and sugar in a pan until the sugar dissolves.

Blitz the other two beets with a spoonful of the pickling liquor until smooth.

Halve the cucumber, remove the seeds and cut one half the cucumber into nice shapes (I like to use a scoop and make little balls). Cover these with the remaining pickling liquor and leave for 10 minutes, then drain.

Slice the other half of the cucumber into very thin half-moon shapes. Season with a little salt and allow to soften for 5 minutes.

Peel the lemon, juice it and place in a pan with the water and honey. Simmer to reduce by two thirds (approximately 30 minutes). Add salt then blitz until fine.

Deep fry the capers at 180°c until crispy, then drain on kitchen towel.

Take the salmon portions out of the liquor, divide the rillettes between them and spread it over the top evenly. Arrange the cucumber scales on top. Drizzle with a little olive oil for shine.

To serve, place a spoon of beet purée just off centre on the plate, splat with the back of a spoon (don't wear white!) then place the dressed salmon on top. Arrange the roast beets, pickled cucumber and crispy capers nicely around the salmon and drizzle over a small amount of lemon purée. Garnish with dill sprigs.

PREPARATION TIME: 45 MINUTES | COOKING TIME: 1 HOUR | SERVES: 4

SHEFFIELD

BORN & BRED

WITH A LONG HISTORY IN SHEFFIELD, AND KEEN SUPPORTER OF LOCAL CHARITIES, HENRY BOOT IS A COMPANY THAT PRIDES ITSELF ON THE PURPOSE, VISION AND VALUES IT LIVES AND WORKS BY.

Henry Boot has maintained a partnership with Whirlow Hall Farm for several years, and is a keen supporter of the charitable work it does. The company regularly sponsors events put on by Whirlow and offers support when possible. In turn, Whirlow Hall Farm provides all the food for the annual summer barbecue hosted by Henry Boot which also raises money for the company's charity of the year.

The strong connection and mutual involvement is partly thanks to how close they are in a literal sense – just up the road – and also a number of people working at Henry Boot who know the charity well on a personal level. The team are proud to support "the brilliant work they do at Whirlow Hall Farm for all the children" and have an ethos that matches the charity's, since "the development of young people in the city is close to our hearts" and lots of apprenticeships are offered to this end.

The company was established over 130 years ago, and is the parent of the Henry Boot Group which is based in Sheffield. A UK leader in property investment and development, land promotion and construction, Henry Boot was founded by the son of a farmer in Heeley and has built a sound reputation over the years with a longstanding presence in its specialist markets.

The team pride themselves on the purpose, vision and values set out by 'The Henry Boot Way' which was created by volunteers from across the Group of Companies. The business uses this to explain how it works and what customers can expect, because the success of the work always comes down to the people who bring their skills and commitment to each project.

Creating long-term value and sustainable growth is the aim that underpins Henry Boot, and this stems from empowering and developing people to produce those results for the company's stakeholders. These include shareholders, employees, pensioners, customers and suppliers. The vision evolved from this goal, as it centres around a trusted reputation, respect for expertise, and being valued for a forward-thinking approach. There are six key values that are integral to all of this and define the company: adaptability, collaboration, delivery, integrity, loyalty, and respect.

THE MOST DELICIOUS TIFFIN

"This recipe is sure to become a family favourite. My mum used to make it for me and my brother and sister, and now I make it for my kids. You might need to make two batches though because it won't be around for long!" – Rachel Taylor, Company Accountant

225g digestive biscuits

115g soft brown sugar

115g butter

3 tbsp cocoa powder

A few drops of vanilla essence

1 egg, beaten

200g milk chocolate

In a large bowl, bash the biscuits with the end of a rolling pin until they are all finely crushed.

Put a saucepan over a medium heat and melt the sugar and butter together until all the sugar has dissolved (you should not be able to feel or see any grains of sugar when running the spoon along the bottom of the saucepan). Take the pan off the heat and then stir in the cocoa powder and vanilla essence. Quickly whisk in the beaten egg until it is combined into the mixture.

Add this mixture to the crushed biscuits and stir well to incorporate all the crumbs. Tip the mixture into a 20cm tin lined with greaseproof paper and press down to get an even surface.

Melt the milk chocolate and pour it over the top of the tiffin base, then place the tin in the fridge to set. Cut into 8 or 12 pieces and enjoy!

PREPARATION TIME: 30 MINUTES, PLUS CHILLING | SERVES: 8-12 (VARIES ON SIZE OF SLICE)

A RECIPE

FOR
SUCCESS

FROM SHEFFIELD TO JERUSALEM, MEZE PUBLISHING HAS PUBLISHED COOK BOOKS WITH FOODIE PEOPLE ALL OVER THE COUNTRY AND BEYOND.

Meze Publishing was formed in 2013 by three publishing professionals: Paul Cocker, Nick Hallam and Phil Turner. They have built a successful Sheffield-based company on the founding aim of producing high quality, beautiful cook books. The team of publishing managers, journalists, graphic designers and photographers – both freelance and in-house – are passionate about good food and drink, and celebrating the places that create it. They offer a creative, professional and personal service for anyone who wants to feature in or produce their own cook book.

The specialist publisher has produced over 40 titles in the well-known regional 'Get Stuck In' series, which began with The Sheffield Cook Book in 2014. These recipe books also act like local guides, thanks to the wide range of businesses that feature in their pages – including cafés, restaurants, producers, distilleries, breweries, farm shops, delis, bars, gastropubs...you name it! – and showcase the culinary landscape of the area. From Cornwall to Glasgow, the regional series continues to be popular across the country, and has even made its way overseas to Amsterdam and Den Haag.

As the business has grown and developed, several award-winning and Michelin-starred chefs have chosen Meze to produce and publish their cook books. These include 2013 MasterChef finalist Adam

Handling as well as 2015's champion Simon Wood – both of whom now have their own chain of successful restaurants – and the two-Michelin-starred chef Daniel Clifford, chef patron of Midsummer House in Cambridge. Other projects have come in the form of a book about making your own dairy-free milks, Plant Milk Power, an eclectic collection of recipes by a North London cooking club, and a celebration of home baking from Jervaulx Abbey Tearoom in North Yorkshire.

Amidst the whirlwind of production, new prospects and regular releases, Meze Publishing was awarded the IPG (Independent Publisher's Guild) Newcomer of the Year award in 2016 and managing director Phil Turner earned The Bookseller's industry accolade of 'Rising Star' during the same year. "Our publishing model is very different from the norm," says Phil. "We structure the deal so that our clients receive the maximum benefit. Over the years we have built-up excellent contacts with retailers and the book trade. Through all of this we've maintained our core belief: to produce high quality, beautiful cook books that sell."

Meze Publishing is proud to be customer-focused and Sheffield-based, so the opportunity to work with Whirlow Hall Farm and produce a book to help support the charity while once again showcasing the city's fantastic food and drink was not one to be missed!

THE MEZE BURGER

The richest, juiciest and most delectable burger to ever grace your plate. Created and cooked regularly by our resident burger aficionado and graphic designer Matt Crowder.

FOR THE SPECIAL SAUCE

200ml mayonnaise

75ml tomato sauce

75ml American mustard

1 tbsp Henderson's Relish

2 tsp paprika

1 tsp salt

50g gherkins, finely minced

1 tbsp gherkin juice

FOR THE HENDO'S CARAMELISED ONIONS

2 large white onions

3 tbsp unsalted butter

1 tbsp fine brown sugar

2 tbsp Henderson's Relish

Salt and pepper

FOR THE CANDIED BACON

7 tbsp fine brown sugar

3 tbsp water

12 slices applewood smoked bacon

FOR THE BURGER PATTIES

800g freshly minced chuck steak, or 20% fat beef mince

TO SERVE

Sesame seeded brioche burger buns

Iceberg lettuce, shredded

Splash of rapeseed oil

4 slices of American cheese

Gherkins, thinly sliced

FOR THE SPECIAL SAUCE

Mix all ingredients together in a bowl and adjust the seasoning to taste.

FOR THE HENDO'S CARAMELISED ONIONS

Peel and halve the onions before thinly slicing. Add the butter to a large pan, and when melted add the onions. Sauté until soft, then add the sugar and Henderson's Relish. Cook for a further 30 to 40 minutes, stirring occasionally until the onions are a dark brown colour and have a slightly jammy texture. Season to taste with salt and black pepper, then cover and keep warm until needed.

FOR THE CANDIED BACON

Preheat the oven to 190°c. Whisk the sugar and water together until they form a glaze. Place the bacon on a foil-lined baking sheet before brushing the glaze liberally over the bacon. Place the bacon into the preheated oven to cook for 20 to 25 minutes. When done, transfer to a plate lined with paper towels so the bacon can dry out and crisp up further.

FOR THE BURGER PATTIES

Weigh out four 200g portions. Roll each into a large ball, without overworking as this will toughen it up. Chill the meatballs and then remove from the fridge at least 20 minutes before cooking.

TO COOK AND SERVE

Get all your condiments and toppings ready before starting any cooking. Lightly butter the brioche buns before toasting in a pan over a low heat. Add a dollop of special sauce to all the cut sides of the burger buns and pile some shredded iceberg lettuce on the bottom half of each bun.

Meanwhile, heat up a flat skillet pan until it is ripping hot, then coat with a very small amount of rapeseed oil.

Season one side of the meatballs with salt and place seasoned side down into the pan, then quickly smash them with a spatula until you have four patties roughly 2cm deep. Turn the heat down to medium-high and cook for 2 minutes on the first side. Do not move the burger during this time!

Flip the burger and cook for 1 minute on the other side before adding a slice of cheese and the caramelised onions to each patty. Add a little water to the pan and cover with a lid. Leave for 1 minute to melt the cheese.

Place the patties into the burger buns, top with a few slices of gherkin and three rashers of candied bacon each, serve and enjoy!

PREPARATION TIME: 20 MINUTES | COOKING TIME: 45 MINUTES | SERVES: 4

WHAT A LOT OF BOTTLE

FAMOUS NOT ONLY FOR ITS WINE BUT ALSO SPIRITS, BEERS AND CIGARS, MITCHELLS WINES PRIDES ITSELF ON ITS INDEPENDENCE, EXTENSIVE RANGE AND GREAT VALUE NOT EASILY FOUND ELSEWHERE, AND THE KNOWLEDGEABLE STAFF WHO MAKE EACH VISIT A UNIQUE EXPERIENCE.

Mitchells is a family business dating back to 1935, and is run today by John Mitchell whose daughter Francesca also works in the shop on Meadowhead, the fourth generation to do so. You might say that the drinks industry runs in the Mitchell family bloodline; John was delighted when Francesca decided to join the business, and many of their relatives worked in the trade before them. John's dad was born and bred in the Wagon and Horses, Millhouses, where his grandfather was landlord, and ran the shop while John's dad was away serving in the Irish Guard during the Second World War. John's great-grandfather owned the Adelphi in Sheffield which was later demolished to make way for the Crucible theatre, and is where Sheffield Wednesday, United and Yorkshire Cricket Club were founded. Even further back down the line of Steel City ancestors is Thomas Boulsover who invented Sheffield plate.

This illustrious history and the Mitchell family commitment to wetting Sheffield's whistle has been recognised in the form of a Lifetime Achievement for John at the Off License News' Drinks Retailing Awards. The shop has also scooped Wine Merchant of the Year twice, as well as the same in the beer and spirit categories, and most recently came second only to Selfridges which as John points out can't be bad! It also holds an impressive selection of Havana cigars and is in fact the second largest cigar retailer in the North.

Mitchells Hop House is the brewery next door, which has produced over 80,000 pints to date! It was a dream come true for John to transform the adjoining property into a brewery to open summer 2016, and to curate his collection of beer-related memorabilia in the upstairs space which alongside being a beer museum also plays host to regular tasting events.

The gin cabinet features over 300 varieties, and represents distilleries from many counties across the UK as well as countries around the world. The whisky collection has also grown significantly to more than 500 varieties, and there are also more than 500 craft beers in stock. The wine is still a mainstay of course, with over 900 different wines to choose from! Mitchells has supplied the annual Whirlow Hall Farm shoot with wine for several years now, and is now supplying beers for events because, as John says, "it is for such a great cause, and we enjoy supporting the charity."

TRIPPET LANE S1

WINE & RECIPE PAIRINGS

WE'VE PICKED OUT SOME OF THE RECIPES FEATURED IN THIS BOOK AND SUGGESTED WINE PAIRINGS FOR THEM, SO YOU CAN TURN ANY MEAL OR SWEET TREAT INTO A SPECIAL OCCASION.

Meze Publishing: The Meze Burger

Without the choice of a nice IPA, grab a glass of red. Pinot Noir, the staple grape of Burgundy, is doing very well in New Zealand, predominantly grown in the cooler southerly regions of Wairarapa, Nelson and Central Otago. The diversity in climate and soils supports a wide range of styles; you will find structure and elegance as well as fruit-driven intensity. This still comprises under 10% of New Zealand's total wine production, so handle with care.

P J Taste: Gooseberry, Honey and Elderflower Fool

The region of Alsace on France's border with Germany predominantly produces white wine due to the German influence. Besides Gewurztraminer, it offers fantastic Riesling which is highly aromatic and, to me, one of the world's best ever grapes. The 40,000 acres in the region produce 150 million bottles, and alongside sampling these great wines a visit to the area is a must.

Chris Beech: Picnic Party

Picnic time calls for fizz, but with Prosecco coming out of our ears why not try something different? 'Cremant De Bourgogne' is an appellation describing the sparkling wines of Burgundy, France. White or rosé in style, they are not so very different from Champagne in taste but have their own very special sparkle.

Seymour Millington: Homemade Sweets

What better tipple to complement a sweet than a pudding wine? Sauterne, a sweet Bordeaux from France, was standard fare back in the 1970s but is expensive today, so why not try a late harvest new world Semillon; the half size bottles offer value for money and it's ideal with marshmallows.

B. Braun: Rainbow Wraps

Chenin Blanc is so versatile; it comes as a dry summer wine or can be offered oaked and aged, similar to Chardonnay. Don't forget the medium style, verging on a slight sweetness, which makes an ideal partner for some fabulous vegetarian and vegan dishes.

Brocco Kitchen: Beef Cheek, Wensleydale and Celeriac Cottage Pie

Wensleydale doesn't need a shy wine, so for ox cheek, try a Malbec. Malbec started life in France as the staple grape of the Cahors, but Argentina are producing some amazing Malbec these days. Ask your wine merchant for a full-bodied Malbec as some are quite a lot lighter in style.

RMS Construction: Stew and Dumplings with Hendo's

A robust red with big tannins goes well with brisket. Why not try one of the wonderful Cabernet Sauvignons coming out of Chile? They have backbone and a long finish to combat the Hendo's.

FRENCH WINE REGIONS

HAVING JOINED OUR FAMILY BUSINESS IN 1967, WHEN WE WERE A BUTCHER'S SHOP WITH AN OFF-LICENCE ATTACHED. THE WINE SELECTION THEN WAS PREDOMINANTLY FRENCH PLUS LOTS OF SWEETER GERMAN WINES. THE 'NEW WORLD' WAS UNHEARD OF; WE HAD A LITTLE FROM SOUTH AFRICA BUT MAINLY FORTIFIED, AND PORTUGAL WAS PORT ONLY. ITALY AND SPAIN WERE JUST STARTING TO PUSH NORTHWARDS, SO MY PAIRINGS FOR THIS BOOK HAD TO BE FRENCH FOR OLD TIMES' SAKE!

Champagne

I've been fortunate enough to stay at Chateau de Saran, the home of Dom Pérignon. The chef de cave was then Richard Geoffroy, who always offered unbelievable food matches with various new and old vintages of their wonderful Champagne. I suggest a glass with breakfast, especially scrambled eggs and mushrooms.

The Lush Loire Valley

The Loire is famous for its Sauvignons, and there are none better than Paul Thomas Les Comtesses Sancerre, a wine we've stocked for over 40 years. Different to the New Zealand style, try this with chargrilled asparagus topped with shavings of Parmesan.

Fine Bordeaux

Bordeaux is the home of Claret and the world's largest fine wine area, offering tannic Cabernet Sauvignons blended with Cabernet Francs and the softer Merlot. These have fantastic appellations including St Emillion, Pomerol, St Estephe, Medoc, Margaux and Pauillac. My mother and father loved pheasant: what a match with a Grand Chateau.

The South West

Cahors has a history of winemaking dating back to the era of ancient Rome, with vines planted as early as 50BC. It produces the Malbec grape which creates 'the black wine', different to the new and upcoming Argentinian Malbec but a must with 30-day old dry-aged ribeye cooked medium-rare.

Alsace

The Hugel family started making wine in 1639 on prime sites in Riquewihr. They produce over one hundred thousand bottles per year. It's their Riesling I particularly admire, having drunk this with Etienne Hugel a few years ago in his cellar while enjoying fresh grilled sole and oysters.

Wonderful Burgundy

Bouchard Pere et Fils was founded in 1731 in Beaune. They purchased Chateau De Beaune in 1820, which is a former royal fortress with deep underground cellars ideal for wine, especially Burgundy's superb reds. From the majestic Pinot Noir grape to Chardonnay, Burgundy is my all-time favourite with a Sunday roast.

The Beaujolais

Many years ago, I visited the king of the Beaujolais, George Duboeuf. In the 1970s Beaujolais was the best-selling French red. Beaujolais Nouveau spoilt this, but it was tremendous fun selling 1000 bottles of the new vintage on the third Thursday in November. Made from the Gamay grape, you can even serve it chilled: a proper picnic wine on a hot day.

Rhone Valley

Syrah, or Shiraz as it's commonly known, E. Guigal Cotes Du Rhône is inexpensive and comes up trumps vintage after vintage. The full-bodied, powerful and peppery character has an easy food match: roasted leg of lamb with savoy cabbage and baby carrots.

Provence

Just chill and enjoy a glass of the wonderful rosé from this area in the south east of France... picture yourself sat on the French Riviera between Cannes and Nice, enjoying a tuna niçoise salad.

Languedoc Roussillon

Vin De Pays d'oc wine stretches from the Spanish border to Provence. With 700,000 acres of vines – more than the whole of Australia – this is the single biggest wine producing area in the world. It's responsible for over a third of France's total wine production. There are lots of different grapes, including the red Corbières and Minervois which are mostly produced by wine cooperatives, and whites from Corbières and Roussillon. A favourite of mine is Fitou with grilled tuna steak: mouth-watering!

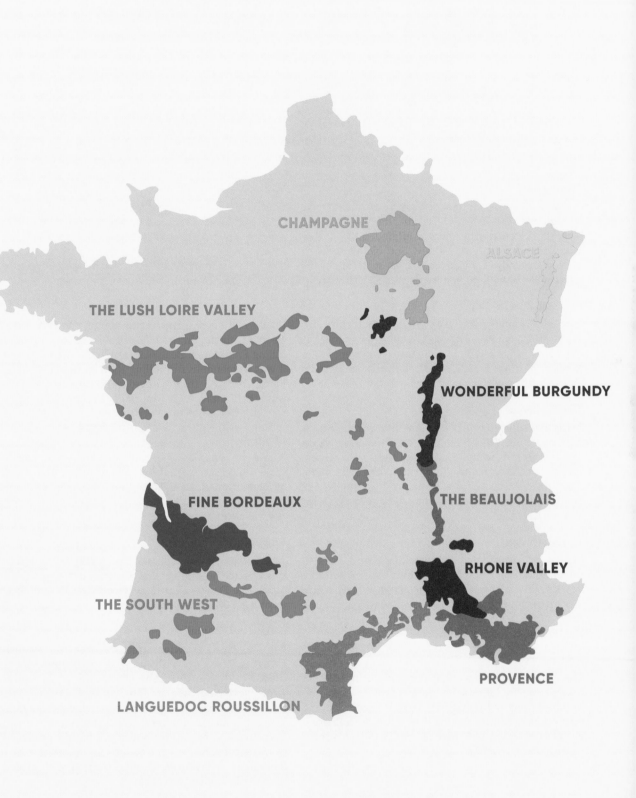

CHAMPAGNE

ALSACE

THE LUSH LOIRE VALLEY

WONDERFUL BURGUNDY

FINE BORDEAUX

THE BEAUJOLAIS

RHONE VALLEY

THE SOUTH WEST

PROVENCE

LANGUEDOC ROUSSILLON

LET THE SUNSHINE IN

NOOSA CAFÉ BAR AIMS TO BRING THE BRUNCHES AND VIBES OF AUSTRALIA'S SUNSHINE COAST TO THE STEEL CITY, PAYING HOMAGE TO A DESTINATION ITS OWNERS LOVE WITH THE PASSION AND KNOWHOW OF EXPERIENCED RESTAURATEURS.

Opened in June 2019, Noosa Café Bar is the brainchild of partners Charlie Curran and Kelly Ware, and an exciting new addition to Sheffield's social scene. The Kelham Island hangout is inspired by the Australian resort of Noosa, where Charlie and Kelly had a fantastic family holiday and loved everything about the place. The café culture there – which invariably means great coffee and great food – has a laid back feel and informal yet friendly service, which they decided to bring back to their home city.

Charlie has been a well-known chef in Sheffield for many years, and previously ran the restaurant Peppercorn with Kelly. The pair are taking some of the things they learnt there into this new venture, including a personality-led approach to staffing and a focus on making the workplace enjoyable for both sides of the pass, by creating a happy environment and ensuring good balance between work and play. Noosa will also use suppliers with whom Charlie has built strong relationships, such as Cafeology whose Sheffield-roasted coffee was served at Peppercorn, alongside bringing Kelham producers on board. "Quality is always our absolute priority," say Kelly and Charlie, "and using these trusted local people means we can be consistently good too."

The café's breakfast and brunch menu is served until late afternoon, while lunch comprises specials that change daily, and there is also a healthy kid's menu that doesn't rely on chips with everything! From soups and sandwiches to on-trend vegan dishes and Asian influences, the food at Noosa is bright and vibrant just like the atmosphere it aims to create. From 4pm onwards the bar aspect is more in evidence, open for locals to pop in and enjoy the sociable vibe and warm welcome. "We want Noosa to have a relaxed quality, and to offer people somewhere to enjoy themselves no matter what they fancy to eat or drink or the time of day," say the owners.

Part of the Noosa ethos is to embrace the community and others who value it, like Whirlow Hall Farm. Sous chef Luke is representing the business at the Sheff's Kitchen competition in 2019, which Charlie won when it was first established. "Those early Chefs Kitchens were great for putting us on the map but of course also raise a lot of money for the charity, which is a fantastic outcome on both sides," says Charlie. "We have lots of ties to Whirlow now and are always happy to work with them."

RAMEN

Ramen is a Japanese noodle broth which is becoming very popular in the UK. It is generally made using a chicken or seafood stock, but can be made without these to make a vegetarian version. Nori and kombu are different types of dried edible seaweed that give great depth of flavour to the broth.

10 chicken wings

2 leeks

3 carrots

2 white onions

1 red onion

1 bunch of spring onions

1 piece of root ginger

2 bulbs of garlic

2 whole chillies

150ml soy sauce

150ml sesame oil

150ml Shaoxing rice wine

2 tsp chilli bean paste

3 tsp salt

3 tsp pepper

1 sheet of nori

1 sheet of kombu

6 dried shitake mushrooms

2½ litres water

TO SERVE

200g egg noodles

1 bell pepper, finely sliced

½ a leek, finely sliced

½ a mooli, finely sliced

12 leaves of pak choi

6 poached eggs

1-2 chillies, finely sliced

1-2 spring onions, finely sliced

6 sprigs of coriander

6 pieces of nori

Roast the chicken wings in a hot oven at about 200°c until golden brown. Meanwhile, peel and roughly chop the leeks, carrots, onions, spring onions, ginger and garlic. Place the roasted chicken wings and prepared veg into a large stock pot with all the other ingredients. Bring slowly to the boil, reduce the heat and simmer very slowly for at least 3 hours. If you have a large slow cooker this process can be done overnight, for up to 12 hours. When the cooking time is up, pass the liquid through a fine sieve or muslin into a bowl so you end up with a clear broth.

TO SERVE

In a clean pan, reheat your base stock and then add the noodles and sliced vegetables. Divide the ramen into six deep bowls, add two leaves of pak choi to each one and then top with a soft poached egg. Garnish the ramen with finely sliced chillies and spring onion, a sprig of fresh coriander, and a piece of nori for each person.

GREEN FINGERS

SUSTAINABLE FOOD HAS ALWAYS BEEN AT THE HEART OF PJ TASTE, AND THEIR FLOURISHING FOREST GARDEN PRODUCING EVERYTHING FROM HONEY TO SOFT FRUIT AND PERENNIAL VEGETABLES EPITOMISES THIS...

PJ taste champions seasonally inspired local food. John and Peter opened their coffee shop on West Street in 2006 where a smoked tofu salad with gluten-free noodles became the best seller. This creativity has characterised their food from the start, and the wide range of options, from office buffets and weddings to spits roasts and wood-fired pizza, really sets the venture apart. Today PJ taste employs a team of dedicated caterers to deliver delicious and innovative food for corporate events and family celebrations all over Sheffield and Derbyshire.

The business is also proud to be developing its own forest garden on the outskirts of the city. Increasingly, this supplies a range of sustainably grown fruit, edible flowers, herbs and salad as well as more unusual perennial vegetables. The plot has wild areas for foraging and plenty of space for the bees which produce PJ taste's own honey. Three wildlife ponds attract a range of flora and fauna such as frogs and toads, ladybirds and dragonflies all of which help to keep insect pests like aphids at controlled levels. "It's all about balance," explains Peter on his approach to managing the two acres of land. "Letting nature get on with it rather than interfering can produce some fantastic results."

In the short time Peter has been using the land to grow sustainably, he has seen huge changes in the health of the soil and plants. Ground cover is provided by plants like Nepalese raspberries and herbs while bushes such as blackcurrants are sheltered by a variety of fruit and nut trees. There are even pear, quince and medlar grafted onto the locally adapted hawthorn which are in turn shaded by tall trees including walnut, alder and lime. Climbing plants like hops grow between and up through all of this, and wild areas of nettles and other 'weeds' are important for biodiversity, as are the wildflower meadows that blossom on unmown lawns.

The edible fruits and the ability to forage in a controlled way inform the menus at PJ taste and are the inspiration for a wealth of dishes all year round. PJ taste want to encourage the idea that this is not a niche way of growing your own, and like Whirlow Hall Farm they believe in the importance of knowing where your food comes from and celebrating what nature has to give us, if we treat it well.

GOOSEBERRY, HONEY AND ELDERFLOWER FOOL

Working with the seasons tends to suggest its own flavour combinations. The ripening of gooseberries in June which follows the blooming of the elderflowers and the chance to harvest spring blossom honey from our bees is a perfect example. Using a good quality yoghurt containing live bacterial cultures arguably makes this a much healthier dish than using the traditional cream, but still exceedingly tasty!

30ml elderflower cordial (see method to make your own)

800g gooseberries, tops and tails snipped off

70g raw blossom honey (or 120g caster sugar, for the same sweetness but not such a good flavour!)

275g thick yoghurt

It's fun to make your own cordial if you have the time, perhaps taking the opportunity to forage for the flowers with your family. Simply leave 10 to 15 heads of elderflower to steep overnight in a sugar syrup made with 300ml of water, 500g of sugar and the juice of a lemon.

Place the gooseberries in a saucepan and add the honey, a splash of water and the elderflower cordial (homemade or bought). Gently cook the gooseberries for 10 to 15 minutes until the fruit softens and the juices run. Drain in a sieve over a bowl to remove any excess juice. (Mix this with some sparkling water for a refreshing drink).

For a completely smooth result, blend all the cooked fruit in a food processor, or keep a quarter back and stir this whole fruit into the purée for a nice variation in texture.

Leave the fruit to cool before folding it into the yoghurt, and then spoon into glasses for serving along with a garnish of your choice, or just as it is. As cooks, we often feel the need to embellish! We have done so here with edible flowers (viola and borage, as they are such bee-friendly flowers) and cubes of our own natural honeycomb coated in chocolate.

PREPARATION TIME: 15 MINUTES, PLUS OVERNIGHT IF MAKING CORDIAL
| COOKING TIME: 10-15 MINUTES | SERVES: 6

SHOUT IT TO THE
RAFTERS ABOUT RAFTERS!

THE ICONIC SHEFFIELD RESTAURANT HAS ENTERED A NEW PHASE THAT'S ALL ABOUT DELIVERING THE BEST GUEST EXPERIENCE IN AN ATMOSPHERE OF ABSOLUTE COMFORT.

You'd be hard pushed to find a Sheffielder who hasn't heard of Rafters, but there's more to discover about the iconic restaurant than many realise. Rafters is co-owned by chef Tom Lawson and front of house manager Alistair Myers, whose philosophy focuses on creating and delivering the very best experiences for their guests. To do this, the kitchen and front of house have to work closely and harmoniously, ensuring the whole package – from the greeting to the desserts – is amazing.

A very significant part of this package is, of course, the food. There are tasting, two course and three course menus at Rafters for anyone to try. Tom has a distinctive style, making each dish stand out with his way of cooking and plating, but at its heart the food is about simply using the best produce in the best way. Herbs, fruit, and vegetables including asparagus and potatoes often come from Tom's own garden which he has been developing over several years. Local products such as Sheffield Honey and Little Mesters also put in appearances, striking a balance with the raw materials Tom and his team like to craft their food out of.

Alistair is a qualified sommelier, and two of his staff are also trained in the art of great wine pairing, so there will always be someone to help you decide whether the wine flight is for you, or which glass to enjoy from hand-picked selection. His skills were put to good use as maître d' at the 2018 final of Whirlow Hall Farm's Sheff's Kitchen; Rafters have since been a supporter of the charity. Alistair is a firm believer that the staff can make or break the 'vibe' of a restaurant, so the service is not only warm and friendly but tailored to each individual diner – not everyone wants the same thing from a meal out, so guests shouldn't be treated exactly the same because it's about what makes them feel most comfortable.

Little details like the padding under the tablecloths and ergonomic cutlery made from Sheffield steel offer extra comfort without even being noticeable. It's the extra care and attention that elevates Rafters, but also what makes Tom and Alistair keen to break down the barrier that means fine dining can all too easily seem intimidating. Rafters welcomes anyone who simply wants to enjoy a fantastic meal out, and underneath the Michelin listings, rosettes and Good Food Guide recommendations it's still Sheffield's own through and through.

GRANARY AND BLACK TREACLE BREAD

We have chosen this bread as it is our most requested recipe, and even if you've never made bread before it's really easy to bake.

FOR THE DOUGH

30g fresh yeast

300g white bread flour

420g seeded brown bread flour (we use organic stone ground flour from Worsborough Water Mill)

22g salt

50g black treacle

60g dark brown sugar

150g chocolate stout

250g tepid water

FOR THE GLAZE

1 egg yolk

10g black treacle

1 tbsp warm water

Mix all the ingredients for the dough together in a food mixer with the dough hook attachment, until the mixture leaves the sides of the bowl. This should take 8 to 10 minutes, or quite a bit longer by hand. Cover the bowl with cling film and prove somewhere warm for 1 hour.

Split the dough into three and roll each piece into a loaf on a floured work surface. Place the loaves on a baking sheet lined with silicon paper.

FOR THE GLAZE

Whisk the egg yolk with the black treacle and one tablespoon of warm water. Brush the glaze over each loaf, then leave them to prove for a further 45 to 60 minutes until doubled in volume.

Bake the loaves in a preheated oven at 200°c for 30 minutes. Allow to cool on wire rack for at least 20 minutes before slicing and tucking in.

PREPARATION TIME: 15 MINUTES, PLUS 2 HOURS PROVING | COOKING TIME: 30 MINUTES | MAKES 3 LOAVES

HOMES IN
SAFE
HANDS

RMS CONSTRUCTION IS A FAMILY-OWNED COMPANY THAT CAN OFFER A WEALTH OF EXPERIENCE AND TOP NOTCH CUSTOMER SERVICE ON BUILDING PROJECTS FROM RENOVATIONS TO NEW BUILDS.

RMS Construction was established in 1986 as a one-man band by Robert Mark Smith. Originally a joiner, Mark – as he is more usually known – put his initials and his conscientious approach into the business, resulting in significant growth over the next few decades. The company now has a team of over 30 people which includes Nikki Smith, head of sales and marketing and Mark's wife, and in-house contractors to ensure the best quality results on every project.

Having moved back into domestic developments from the commercial market, RMS works on a range of projects including but not limited to new builds, renovations, loft conversions, extensions, shop fittings and restaurant refurbishments. What sets the team apart is the customer service they provide with every undertaking no matter who the client is or what scale the building is on. Mark has always project managed all projects and understands the importance of allowing clients to feel comfortable and assured while their house or business is filled with construction crews!

Combined with more than 40 years of experience, this approach makes RMS stand out in the industry. The company has never grown complacent though, instead continuing to evolve with ambitions to become the best of its kind in the Sheffield region. RMS has worked within the Steel City, Chesterfield, Derbyshire and the surroundings areas, and in 2018 the company was named Best New Home and Renovation Builder for South Yorkshire and Derbyshire by Build Magazine in its Real Estate and Property Awards. Mark, Nikki and the team aspire to earn more accolades for RMS in the near future.

The ethos which underpins the company extends to supporting other local business and charities like Whirlow Hall Farm. "It's just amazing that Whirlow exists to support children who might have been labelled 'troublesome' but actually just need that extra bit of time and attention that this charity can give them," says Nikki. "We should all go out of our way to support them because it's wonderful work they are doing. Plus, it's a great place for families to visit – our three year old loves going to the farm for the day!"

GRANNY SMITH'S STEW AND DUMPLINGS WITH HENDO'S

This is serious stew and dumplings! In fact, we would argue that this recipe is the best in existence. Simple, cheap ingredients with some traditional touches combine to create our 4th generation Smith family recipe. The dumplings are not for the faint hearted by any stretch but perfect after a hard day's 'graft' or for a Sunday lunch, and very fitting for a family full of builders. We invite you to try it wholeheartedly but must insist it be served with lashings of 'Endo's (Henderson's Relish)... it'll stick your ribs together.

FOR THE STEW

1kg beef brisket

1kg carrots

1 whole turnip

3-4 large white onions

2-3 sticks of celery

2 beef stock cubes

1 chicken stock cube

300ml boiling water

Salt and pepper

2 tbsp plain flour

2 tbsp gravy granules (we use Bisto)

FOR THE DUMPLINGS

500g self-raising flour

200g shredded suet

Pinch of salt

FOR THE STEW

Preheat the oven to 180°c. Brown the beef brisket in a large casserole dish – big enough to bathe in – then chop all the veg into chunky pieces and add them to the beef once browned. Mix thoroughly.

Dissolve the stock cubes in the boiling water and add the stock to the meat and vegetables. Top up with cold water until all the ingredients are just covered. Bring to the boil, season generously with salt and pepper, then cover the casserole dish and place the stew into the preheated oven. Leave to cook for 2 to 2 and a half hours, stirring half way through.

Combine the plain flour and gravy granules in a small bowl, then gradually add cold water while stirring to make a thick paste. When the stew is cooked, remove it from the oven and stir in the paste.

FOR THE DUMPLINGS

Mix all the ingredients together in a large bowl. Gradually add cold water until the mixture comes together. Form six to eight cricket ball sized dumplings (or smaller ones for the non-builders out there) using your hands. Place the dumplings into the stew on the stove top and bring to the boil.

Once the stew is boiling, place it back into the oven to cook uncovered for a further 45 minutes, or until the dumplings have formed a delicious crust on the top.

Serve with Henderson's Relish, and plenty of it. Yummy!

PREPARATION TIME: 20 MINUTES | COOKING TIME: 2½ TO 3 HOURS
| SERVES: 6 WELL OR 10 CONSERVATIVELY

NO
GREASY CHIP BUTTIES HERE

SOMETHING OF A LOCAL CELEBRITY WHEN IT COMES TO SHEFFIELD'S FOOD SCENE, SEYMOUR MILLINGTON IS BRINGING HIS CATERING EXPERIENCE AND PASSION FOR GOOD FOOD TO SHEFFIELD UNITED'S STADIUM.

Seymour Millington trained at Sheffield College and has catered for some of the biggest names in politics, television and sport during his varied and distinguished career. He has now taken on the role of head chef at Sheffield United Football Club with the caterers Levy UK, following a move into stadium event catering that keeps him busy all year round. "There is a lot more out there than a pie before a football match," he says, "because that only happens about 19 times a year in the league, plus hopefully a good cup run, and the rest of the time we cook for all sorts of occasions including weddings, conferences, parties, you name it."

Good fresh food is the key to any successful catering, even on such a large scale, and Seymour is a firm believer that chefs should absolutely be cooking from scratch as much as possible. Local produce is important, and so are regional staples which give Seymour his inspiration for the menus he creates in advance of the matches. For visiting teams, the meals will often feature an elegant interpretation of a classic dish from their area – a reinvented Eccles cake or hotpot for Manchester United, for example – and include Seymour's personal take on the flavours and ingredients connected to that region.

The team of ten to twelve chefs work incredibly hard behind the scenes to bring these menus to life, across all the different levels of catering a stadium offers. To feed every supporter on match day, this means providing the big restaurant with a four course dinner, another with a luxurious buffet, private dining for those in the boxes, and the rest in the stands, once or twice a week throughout the season. The chefs also factor in dietary requirement and allergies, making all the soups and sauces gluten-free and aiming to create something that everyone can eat, rather than separate meals which could slow down service.

Seymour's management skills and dedication to getting every last detail right are well placed in this sector of the culinary world, and have also seen him crowned winner of local competitions including Sheff's Kitchen in 2018. Seymour is a keen supporter of Whirlow Hall Farm: "it's a fantastic charity, and I like to do anything that I can to help. My daughters did a bake sale at their school to raise money for Whirlow, I'm always excited to be involved their initiatives...it's something I'll always be part of."

TONY
CURRIE
STAND

PULL

HOMEMADE SWEETS

As a young chef one of the first areas I worked on was pastry; these recipes have stuck with me and will always be used. They are very easy to do and will definitely impress!

FOR THE MARSHMALLOWS

Makes 25 portions

600g sugar

125ml water

3 egg whites

10 leaves of gelatine

5-6 tbsp icing sugar, for dusting

5-6 tbsp cornflour, for dusting

RUM & RAISIN FUDGE

Makes 20 portions

595g sugar

510g double cream

130g glucose

½ a shot of rum

50g raisins

HOMEMADE FRUIT PASTILLES

Makes 20 portions

500g raspberry coulis

500g caster sugar

30g pectin

½ lemon, juiced

Caster sugar, for dusting

FOR THE HONEYCOMB

Makes 25 portions

100g honey

650g sugar

120ml water

250g glucose

30g bicarbonate of soda

FOR THE MARSHMALLOW

Put the sugar and water into a small saucepan over a medium heat. Start to slowly whisk the egg whites either in a stand mixer or with a hand held electric whisk until just starting to foam. Soften the gelatine in cold water. Combine the icing sugar and cornflour in a separate bowl.

Heat the sugar until it reaches 140°c then add the gelatine, making sure to squeeze out any excess water first. Slowly pour the sugar mixture onto the egg whites while still whisking. Turn the whisk up to full speed and whisk until the mixture has cooled to room temperature.

Place the marshmallow into a piping bag and pipe your preferred shapes onto a tray dusted with the cornflour and icing sugar mixture, then dust a little more on top to stop them sticking together.

FOR THE RUM & RAISIN FUDGE

Place all ingredients except the raisins in a large saucepan. Place the raisins in a mixing bowl. Boil the mixture in the pan until the core temperature reaches 118°c then pour it onto the raisins. Beat everything together using a slow setting on a mixer with the paddle attachment.

Once the mixture has thickened and cooled, transfer into a shallow tray lined with greaseproof paper. When cold, wrap the fudge tightly and refrigerate for at least 6 hours. Cut into your desired shapes and enjoy!

FOR THE HOMEMADE FRUIT PASTILLES

Place all the ingredients in a saucepan and bring to the boil while stirring constantly until the mixture reaches 110°c. Pour it through a strainer into a tray at least 1cm deep and lined with cling film. Leave to cool, then once the mixture is cold wrap the tray tightly and refrigerate overnight. Cut the fruit pastilles into your desired shape and roll gently in caster sugar.

FOR THE HONEYCOMB

Place all the ingredients except the bicarbonate of soda in a very large saucepan. Boil until the mixture reaches 155°c then take off heat and immediately whisk in the bicarbonate of soda, which will activate and make the mixture rise and foam up. Carefully pour the honeycomb into a tray lined with greaseproof paper then leave to cool and set. Break into whatever size pieces you like.

AN ESTATE OF MIND FOR
THE NEXT GENERATION

THE SPENCER FAMILY HAS A VERY PERSONAL CONNECTION WITH WHIRLOW HALL FARM THAT EXTENDS ACROSS THREE GENERATIONS AND, LIKE THEIR LONGSTANDING ESTATE AGENTS, IS FIRMLY GROUNDED IN SHEFFIELD.

Nicola Spencer, owner of the well-established family business Spencer. The Estate Agent, used to visit Whirlow Hall Farm almost every day as a child, with her parents, grandparents and after school with her brother. They lived within walking distance, and it became a constant in her life, whether she was excited to see some newborn piglets or enjoying the scenic path through the fields which connected her parent's house with the farm. Today, Whirlow is still a big part of Nicola's life as she takes her own children there – four year old twins who especially love the petting corner – and has family days out with her mum and dad, just as they did when she was young.

It's important to Nicola that her children are able to get lots of fresh air and connect with nature as she did, but also to understand the reality of the food we eat as people generally become more distanced from its origins. By meeting the animals and learning about how they become food for sale on the butcher's counter, or in a breakfast cooked at the café, children can reconnect with what they eat and better appreciate the quality and intrinsic value of the food. Education like this is a key aspect of the charitable work done by the Trust, something which all children can benefit from, but especially those coming from disadvantaged backgrounds or with learning disabilities.

Part of what Nicola aspires to, both as a mum and in her business, is setting a good example. She was instilled with the work ethic displayed by her parents after her mum and dad established Spencer in 1993, and when they retired and Nicola bought out the family business in 2011 she wanted to offer the same inspiration and good future prospects for her own children. "Loving your job is about loving where you live as well as the work you do, and I think giving back to the community you're based in is a big part of that," she says.

For the Spencers, both family life and work are grounded in Sheffield just like the Whirlow Hall Farm Trust. Both recognise the importance of community and of providing the education and outdoor space that seems simple but can be fundamental for children and their families, creating relationships and life lessons that carry across the generations.

HONEY CAKE

I would love to tell you how to make this, but the truth is that honey cake is a favourite recipe from my childhood that my mum always used to make for me, so I have had to rope her in to help out!

150g butter

100g soft brown sugar

150ml clear honey

1 tbsp milk

2 eggs

200g self-raising flour

A few flaked almonds

Preheat the oven to 180˚c. Grease and line a 27½ by 17½cm tin with greaseproof paper.

Put the butter, sugar, honey and milk in a pan and stir over a low heat until the sugar dissolves. Leave the mixture to cool, then gradually beat in the eggs. Lastly, fold in the flour. Pour the mixture into the prepared tin and sprinkle the top with flaked almonds.

Bake the cake in the preheated oven for 30 to 35 minutes until well risen and slightly shrinking back from the tin around the edges. Turn out, remove the paper, and leave to cool on a wire rack.

To serve, cut the cake into 16 pieces. Store in a tin.

PREPARATION TIME: 25 MINUTES | COOKING TIME: 30-35 MINUTES | SERVES: 16

FROM

SEEDLING
TO BLOOM

OPENED BY A PARENT WITH THE AIM OF PROVIDING THE VERY BEST CHILDCARE, SUNFLOWER CHILDREN'S CENTRE IS A PLACE TO LEARN AND PLAY UNDER THE CARE OF COMMITTED STAFF IN FLEXIBLE SESSIONS.

Sunflower Children's Centre was established in 2002 by Karen Simpkin to provide exceptional childcare in a learning environment. The Centre aims to be 'a great place to grow' with an emphasis on nurturing and caring for the children, and this ethos developed in the most natural way from becoming a parent. Having been made redundant while on maternity leave and then unable to find a suitable nursery, Karen decided she would create a perfect solution for her daughter and of course benefit the many other children who now come to Sunflower, from as nearby as the school next door to all corners of Sheffield.

With various clubs and sessions available during and outside of term time, the centre has a number of unique spaces to cater for newborns up to 8-year-olds including Sheffield's only bespoke outdoor classroom, an indoor sensory room, garden, musical centre, a 'mud kitchen' for getting messy and large play yard for lots of running around! Exciting spaces to play and learn from the basis of Sunflower's approach to childcare, which

is delivered by a management team who work really closely and are very committed to Karen's ethos as well as bringing new ideas into the business.

Flexibility when it comes to childcare options for both staff and parents is what really sets Sunflower Children's Centre apart, as Karen believes being as user friendly as possible is crucial to providing the best childcare for everyone. Making improvements is a continual process at the centre, so internal developments are always ongoing and the drive to keep getting better is still at the core.

Karen was keen to work with a local venture that was charitable and relevant to children, so supporting Whirlow Hall Farm – a place she took her daughter to many times and still enjoys a weekend brunch at! – was a perfect fit for Sunflower Children's Centre. They hope to interact more in the future with Whirlow to make parents aware of what a great place it is for families and celebrate the shared values that exist to help children grow and flourish.

FROSTED CUPCAKES

"I used to bake these cupcakes with my mum when I was a little girl, so I know this recipe is suitable for all ages to try. It's quick, easy and really tasty!" – Louise Tribe

FOR THE SPONGE

200g unsalted butter

200g caster sugar

4 eggs

200g self-raising flour

FOR THE FROSTING

200g butter, softened

450g icing sugar, sifted

60ml fresh milk

3-4 drops of vanilla essence (optional)

FOR THE SPONGE

Preheat the oven to 180°c and place cupcake cases in a 12 hole baking tray.

Mix the butter and caster sugar together until light and fluffy. Add the eggs one at a time along with 50 grams of flour, beating after each addition. Once you have incorporated all the eggs and flour, divide the mixture evenly between the cases and place the tray in the oven for 16 to 18 minutes. Once the cupcakes are golden in colour and firm but springy to the touch, remove them from the oven and leave to cool on a wire rack.

FOR THE FROSTING

While the cupcakes are cooling, prepare the frosting. Beat the butter, icing sugar and milk together until fluffy then add 3 or 4 drops of vanilla essence if you are including it. Fill a piping bag with the frosting and pipe swirls on top of the cupcakes. Decorate however you like!

PREPARATION TIME: 10-15 MINUTES | COOKING TIME: 16-18 MINUTES | MAKES: 12

GIVE US A WHIRL

WHIRLOWBROOK HALL IS A BEAUTIFUL STONE-BUILT MANOR HOUSE ON THE EDGE OF THE PEAK DISTRICT, OPERATED BY VINE HOTELS WHO RUN SEVERAL OTHER VENUES AND HOTELS IN THE AREA.

Whirlowbrook Hall was originally a family manor house, set in 39 acres of parkland which is accessible to the public. Once you've discovered the beautiful venue, it's hard to forget its unique character. The entire place can be hired out exclusively, depending on numbers, for weddings, parties big and small, corporate events, business meetings...you name it, Whirlowbrook Hall can almost certainly host it! The location makes it easily accessible from Chesterfield and Sheffield, plus the Peak District is on the doorstep so there's no shortage of natural beauty around.

The building itself embraces these stunning surroundings, letting in the light and showcasing the incredible views across the park from many large windows in the individual rooms. One of these houses the well-stocked bar, which now features English wines amongst its selection. The décor keeps some of the original features throughout the venue, and is also neutral enough to be decorated in whatever style suits the occasion being hosted.

This ethos of flexibility also applies to the catering at Whirlowbrook Hall. The team are led by experienced head chef Alex Fretwell, who works with guests of the venue to create their menus. Food can be served as sharing platters or as a sit down meal with table service, and is freshly prepared in kitchens within the hall. They have ensured there is a strong vegan offering, and try to source produce as locally as possible, so quality and accessibility are always a priority.

Vine Hotels, who operate Whirlowbrook Hall, are experts in managing this kind of venue, as they have a growing portfolio based in Sheffield, with four other hotels or venues across the city and two more further afield. "The hotels and venues under Vine Hotels' umbrella are run to a high standard and have fantastic teams of people working for them, who are very good at what they do and really understand customers," says Alex. They are also members of the Whirlow Hall Farm Trust's 480 Club, which runs events throughout the year. Being locally based, Vine Hotels likes to support charitable work in the area, as well as running beautiful venues to high standards for people to enjoy.

PAN FRIED SCALLOPS, PEA PURÉE, CRISPY CHICKEN SKIN, PARMESAN

This dish from Whirlowbrook Hall is one of our favourites; it's popular with guests and the chef and his team love preparing it. It's a beautiful, tasty dish that is easy to make at home, and your dinner companions are sure to love it too!

2 large scallops

50g chicken skin

Salt and pepper

1 shallot

10ml olive oil

300g peas

100ml water

50g butter

15g Parmesan

Using a sharp knife, prepare the scallops by slowly pulling away the meat away from the shell. Once the scallops have come away from the shells, place them on kitchen roll to dry.

Press the chicken skin between two non-stick trays for a minute to ensure they are flat, then season with salt and pepper. Place the skins on a tray and cook in the oven for 10 minutes at 180°c. Remove and leave to cool, then break into shards.

Heat a saucepan on the hob while you roughly chop the shallot. Once the pan starts to smoke, add the oil and shallot. Keep everything moving with a wooden spoon to stop any colour developing on the shallot.

Once the shallot is soft, add the peas and water. Bring to a rapid boil, then remove the pan from the heat and add the butter.

Once the butter has melted, blend the mixture into a purée with a hand-held blender then pass the purée through a sieve to get it really smooth.

Season with salt and pepper.

Grate the Parmesan onto a chopping board ready for plating.

Heat a non-stick frying pan and when it's smoking add a splash of oil and swirl it around to cover the base of the pan.

Season the scallops with salt and pepper, then place them into the pan. Cook for 1 minute, then gently turn them over and cook on the opposite side for a further 1 minute, bearing in mind that the timings may differ slightly depending on the size of the scallops.

They should be golden and springy to the touch when ready; overcooked scallops will be tough and rubbery.

Spoon the purée onto two serving plates, place the scallops on top with chicken skin on the side and garnish with the Parmesan. Bon appetite!

PREPARATION TIME: 15 MINUTES | COOKING TIME: APPROX. 20 MINUTES | SERVES: 2

MAKING A DIFFERENCE

SHEFFIELD VULCAN ROTARY CLUB IS PART OF ROTARY INTERNATIONAL WITH A WORLDWIDE MEMBERSHIP WHO STRIVE TO MAKE A DIFFERENCE LOCALLY, NATIONALLY AND INTERNATIONALLY.

The work that members of Sheffield Vulcan Rotary Club do is very varied, ranging from a classic car show to helping young people with mock interviews in schools. They even have their very own fund-raising rock 'n' roll band. The club was established in 1979 but the oldest Rotary club in Sheffield was formed nearly 100 years ago. There are over 100 men and women members of the three clubs in the city, attending weekly meetings and lending their time to projects throughout the year. The clubs in Sheffield provide huge opportunities for those interested in joining and for the businesses, charities, organisations and people who benefit from their work.

Rotarians have been involved with Whirlow Hall Farm since the beginning. As a longstanding supporter of the charity, the club helps to provide car parking for events throughout the year. You might also see members at the Sheffield Half Marathon, giving out finisher packs, or working on their long-term project in Beauchief Gardens where significant restoration is underway to transform the previously neglected green space. Much tree and roadside bulb planting is carried out by Rotarians in the city who also organise big events such as Music in the Gardens and the Motor Show.

The Vulcan Club also provides the logistics for Operation Christmas Child – which sends shoeboxes of gifts and necessities around the world to disadvantaged young people. Each year it arranges the collection of around 25,000 shoeboxes within South Yorkshire.

Alongside the practical help it can offer close to home, Vulcan Rotary is involved in the Rotary International Polio Vaccination Programme in partnership with the Bill Gates Foundation. This has almost succeeded in eliminating polio worldwide, and is just one example of how the club works in tandem with over a million members worldwide as part of The Rotary Foundation, one of the biggest and oldest international charities. People who join the club also benefit from staying active, doing rewarding work, helping others, enjoying a wide variety of activities and being part of a fellowship that welcomes men and women from all over the area.

The club always encourages anyone who is interested to make contact via its website, come along to a few meetings and get a feel for how it all works, or simply have a chat with other Rotarians at the many events they can be found organising, supporting and fundraising for Sheffield and beyond.

INDIAN CHICKEN

This is a family recipe, passed down through three generations. It is especially popular with the younger grandchildren, as an introduction to more spicy food. It is very easy and quick to make and relies mainly on store cupboard ingredients. You can also make a vegetarian version of this recipe, substituting chunks of roasted butternut squash for the cooked chicken. It is equally delicious!

25g butter

2 large onions, finely chopped

1 tbsp medium curry powder

¼ tsp ground ginger

1 can (295g) condensed cream of celery soup

150ml milk

25g sultanas

3 tbsp mango chutney

Salt and pepper

900g cooked chicken breast, cut into chunks

150ml soured cream

Heat the butter in a large frying pan and add the onions when it has melted. Cook until the onions are soft and golden. Add the curry powder and ground ginger, then cook for a few minutes longer. Add the soup, milk, sultanas and chutney, then mix and bring to the boil.

Take off the heat, season the sauce with salt and pepper then add the cooked chicken. Return to the heat and simmer gently for 15 minutes.

Stir in the soured cream, then serve with boiled rice and peas or salad.

PREPARATION TIME: 10 MINUTES | COOKING TIME: 25 MINUTES | SERVES: 6

DIRECTORY

THESE GREAT BUSINESSES HAVE SUPPORTED THE MAKING OF
THIS BOOK; PLEASE SUPPORT AND ENJOY THEM.

ANT MARKETING

Antenna House
St Mary's Gate
Sheffield
S2 4QA
Telephone: 0114 2780555
Website: www.antmarketing.com

Ant Marketing was Sheffield's first telemarketing agency, and now at 30 years old has evolved into its largest multi-channel contact centre.

B. BRAUN MEDICAL LTD.

Thorncliffe Park
Brookdale Road
Sheffield
S35 2PW
Telephone: 0114 2259000
Website: www.bbraun.co.uk

Find us on social media @BBraunUK

B. Braun is one of the world's leading manufacturers of medical devices and pharmaceutical products and services.

BIRKDALE SCHOOL

Oakholme Road
Sheffield
S10 3DH
Telephone: 0114 2668408
Website: www.birkdaleschool.org.uk

Birkdale School is an independent day school for children aged 4 to 18. Birkdale offers the highest academic standards, nurturing children to be the best they can be.

BLEND KITCHEN

Wards Exchange
197 Ecclesall Road
Sheffield
S11 8HW
Telephone: 07468417353
Website: www.blendcookeatshare.com

Café and restaurant providing training and employment opportunities to people who don't always get them, serving seasonally influenced, locally sourced and globally inspired food.

BROCCO KITCHEN

92 Brocco Bank
Sheffield S11 8RS
Telephone: 0114 2661233
Website: www.brocco.co.uk

Cosy neighbourhood kitchen in multi-award winning boutique hotel, specialising in modern British food with a Nordic twist. Michelin Plate winner 2018 and 2019.

BUTCHER & CATCH

199-203 Whitham Road
Broomhill
Sheffield
S10 2SP
Telephone: 0114 2631304
Website: www.butcherandcatch.co.uk

Modern British restaurant, serving the very best locally reared meats from Sheffield and South Yorkshire alongside amazing seasonal fish caught around our shores.

BEECHES OF WALKLEY

290-296 South Road
Walkley
Sheffield
S6 3TE
Telephone: 0114 2313018/0114 2340066
Website: www.wedoliver.com

We are here to bring local farm produce to our local inner city community. Support Local.

CHRIS BEECH QUALITY MEATS

370 Fulwood Road
Ranmoor
Sheffield
S10 3TG
Telephone: 0114 2302114
Website: www.wedoliver.com

CMS

1 South Quay
Victoria Quays
Sheffield
S2 5SY
Telephone: 0114 2794000
Website: www.cms.law

One of the world's largest leading law firms with offices in more than 70 locations across 42 countries worldwide, including a long-established presence in Sheffield.

HENRY BOOT PLC

Banner Cross Hall
Ecclesall Road South
Sheffield
S11 9PD
Telephone: 0114 2555444
Website: www.henryboot.co.uk

Sheffield-based company that prides itself on the purpose, vision and values it lives and works by, specialising in property investment and development, land promotion and construction.

MITCHELLS WINE MERCHANTS

352-354 Meadowhead
Sheffield
S8 7UJ
Telephone: 0114 2745587/0114 2740311
Email: info@mitchellswine.co.uk
Find us on social media @MitchellsWines

Well established specialist drinks retailer serving Sheffield since 1935, micro-brewery, Havana cigar specialist and wholesaler to the restaurant trade.

MEZE PUBLISHING

Unit 1b
2 Kelham Square
Sheffield
S3 8SD
Telephone: 0114 2757709
Website: www.mezepublishing.co.uk
Find us on social media @MezePublishing

Specialists in designing, producing and publishing beautiful books. With clients varying from family-run businesses to Michelin-starred chefs and children's book authors.

NOOSA CAFÉ BAR

1b Alma Street
Kelham Island
Sheffield
S3 8RY
Telephone: 0114 2726836
Website: www.noosacafebar.co.uk

A taste of the Sunshine Coast in the Steel City.

PJ TASTE LTD

54 Staniforth Road
Sheffield
S9 3HB
Telephone: 0330 0431954 (Catering Bookings)
Website: www.pjtaste.co.uk

Championing seasonally inspired local food, with catering for any event and menus informed by produce from our own forest garden.

RAFTERS RESTAURANT

220 Oakbrook Road
Sheffield
S11 7ED
Telephone: 0114 2304819
Website: www.raftersrestaurant.co.uk
Find us on Instagram @raftersrestaurant on Facebook @Rafters Restaurant Sheffield and Twitter @Rafterss11

Iconic Sheffield restaurant that welcomes anyone who simply wants to enjoy a fantastic meal out.

RMS CONSTRUCTION LTD

23 Paddock Way
Dronfield
S18 2FE
Telephone: 01246 417125
Website: www.rmsconstruction.co.uk

Family-owned domestic and commercial building company, offering a wealth of knowledge and experience spanning several generations.

SEYMOUR MILLINGTON

Email: Millington-s@sky.com
Find me on Instagram @sey_millington and on Twitter @Sey_chef

Head Chef for Levy at Sheffield United, and seasoned member of Sheffield's culinary scene.

SPENCER. THE ESTATE AGENT

469 Ecclesall Road
Sheffield
S11 8PP
Telephone: 0114 2683682
Website: SpencersEstateAgents.co.uk

Family-run estate agent also specialising in property and block management, new home and development advice throughout Sheffield.

SUNFLOWER CHILDREN'S CENTRE

21 Carter Hall Road
Sheffield
S12 3HS
Telephone: 0114 2657000
Website: www.sunflowerchildrenscentre.co.uk

Providing exceptional childcare in a learning environment, with exciting spaces for play and highly qualified staff to nurture children from seedlings to sunflowers!

WHIRLOWBROOK HALL

Whirlowbrook Park
Ecclesall Road South
Sheffield S11 9QD
Telephone: 0114 2366142
Website: www.whirlowbrook.co.uk

Whirlowbrook Hall is a stunning venue in Sheffield that offers the perfect blend of charm, tradition and modern elegance.

SHEFFIELD VULCAN ROTARY CLUB

Abbeydale Sports Club
Abbeydale Road South
Sheffield
S17 3LJ
Meets at 6.30pm on Tuesday evenings
Email: secretary@vulcanrotary.org.uk

Sheffield Vulcan Rotary Club is part of Rotary International with a worldwide membership who strive to make a difference locally, nationally and internationally.